CU00900876

**Community Care
Practice Handbooks**

General Editor: Martin Davies

Sex and the Social Worker

Community Care Practice Handbooks

General Editor: Martin Davies

Sex and the Social Worker

Leonard Davis

HEINEMANN EDUCATIONAL BOOKS
LONDON

Heinemann Educational Books Ltd
22 Bedford Square, London WC1B 3HH
LONDON EDINBURGH MELBOURNE AUCKLAND
HONG KONG SINGAPORE KUALA LUMPUR NEW DELHI
IBADAN NAIROBI JOHANNESBURG
EXETER (NH) KINGSTON PORT OF SPAIN

British Library Cataloguing in Publication Data

Davis, Leonard
    Sex and the social worker.—(Community care
    practice handbooks; 14)
    1. Social service and sex
    I. Title   II. Series
    306.7′024362   HV41

    ISBN 0-435-82263-2

Cover photograph by Nick Oakes
Typeset by the Castlefield Press, Moulton, Northampton
and printed by Biddles Ltd, Guildford, Surrey

Contents

Preface

Over the years I have from time to time written articles on those aspects of human sexuality having particular relevance for social work practice. The response to my writing has often been considerable: from individuals wishing to share problems; from residential staff against whom allegations have been made; and from staff groups wanting to improve their knowledge and skills. I, too, have grown in understanding through these exchanges as the most complex issues were presented and analysed. Some case examples have, as a result, already been used elsewhere and I am grateful to the Editors of *The British Journal of Social Work* and *Social Work Today* for permission to develop themes from published material, notably, 'Touch, sexuality and power in residential settings' (*The British Journal of Social Work*, vol. 5, no. 4); and a number of contributions to *Social Work Today*.

I am also grateful to the Pergamon Press for kindly allowing me to expand ideas originally expressed in a chapter I wrote for a book edited by Ronald Walton and Doreen Elliott, *Residential Care: A Reader in Current Theory and Practice* (1980); to Elizabeth Gerard of Liverpool for an extract from her placement study; and to Dr Eric Trimmer and his publishers for permission to use a case example from his book *Understanding Anxiety in Everyday Life* (Allen & Unwin, 1970). The contributions of social workers and clients must, for obvious reasons, remain anonymous. All case material has been subjected to social disguise, and the names in the book are fictitious.

Peter Righton, formerly Director of Social Work Studies at the National Institute for Social Work, willingly read the draft manuscript, and made many valuable and challenging suggestions.

LEONARD DAVIS
January 1983

1 Sex and Social Work

It would have been too easy to call this book *Sex and Social Work* as if sex, an aspect of human existence central to a great deal of the work undertaken by field and residential social workers day by day, could be isolated and distanced from the thoughts, feelings and practice of the individuals involved. It can never be viewed in this way. Sex is as much part of the social worker as it is of the client or resident. *Sex and the Social Worker* is based on this assumption, emphasising the fact that the sexual values and sexual attitudes of social workers affect the decisions they make and their reactions to the people they work with, notably in exchanges where sex is identified by one or both parties as an area of concern but also in exchanges where, on the surface, it is not an issue.

Most of the topics in this book – from working with the sexual needs of physically handicapped people to comments on 'victims' and 'offenders' in residential settings – provide huge subjects for discussion in their own right, and it is not possible to plumb the depths of the varied aspects of human sexuality in a short book. In many ways, social workers' responses and attitudes differ over time, for example with age, experience and training. Gradually they evolve their own styles of working and codes of conduct. This book is intended to help them assess their present approaches to practice, and perhaps to enable them to reaffirm and realign a number of basic principles.

I know that what is written will sometimes be regarded as controversial. However, values are changing, and who can say how the 'sexual human being' will appear at the turn of the century? Frames of reference also change, but one thing remains true: each response to the sexuality of a client or resident says something about the social worker and, at the same time, helps or hinders a man, woman, boy or girl in the development or expression of what for most people is a fundamental, vigorous and far-reaching force within his or her physical and emotional make-up.

Personal and professional
In the face of the sexuality of clients or residents, social workers are confronted with their personal and professional sexual selves. Moulded over time, their values and attitudes will have gradually crystallised as a result of their sexual development and experiences:

as children, as adolescents and as adults. In common with other human beings they will keep locked within them vivid memories of their first sexual exchanges with another person, of exploratory sex play as a child and of early sexual arousal in the company of the same or the opposite sex.

Married, single, separated, widowed or divorced, male or female, social workers – with or without children – will have had a range of satisfactions and dissatisfactions from sexual activities, some people finding comfort, indescribable pleasure and fulfilment of their physical, emotional and sometimes spiritual beings, others becoming embittered, frustrated and even nauseated by sexual exchanges, or the thought of them, with same-sex or opposite-sex partners. Their lives will have been affected by their own sexual orientation, whether heterosexual or homosexual. Religious up-bringing and beliefs, too, play an important part in attitudes towards sex. Social workers are influenced by the way that sex and sex education were handled in their own families as they grew up. They may have struggled for a long while with strong and com-pelling fantasies. A number may themselves have been subjected to sexual abuse during their formative years.

In living as members of families some social workers will have observed and been forced to acknowledge the emerging sexuality of their own children. They will have had to cope with any feelings that this may have brought out in them, either regarding their own incestuous desires or the reality of their children's sexual conduct, for example, when they first become aware that they are engaging in sex play, are masturbating or, as adolescents, are having sexual intercourse with their boyfriends or girlfriends.

In all these respects the experiences of social workers, residential and field, do not differ from the rest of the population. The accumulation of sexual experience and the quality of their present sexual relationships will affect to varying degrees their attitudes towards sex and consequently their responses and initiatives as social workers. As sexual beings social workers will have feelings and opinions about a number of issues, for instance contraception; abortion; oral sex; venereal disease; sex and physically handi-capped people; lesbianism; pornography; sex and the under-16s; anal intercourse; sex and mentally handicapped people; prosti-tution. They will react in different ways to the sexual abuse of children: by a member of a child's family; by a friend of the child or family; by a non-related person in a position of authority over the child; or by a complete stranger. In each instance they may make a distinction between violent and non-violent sexual contact.

Setting aside at least part of their personal sexual selves may often be difficult for social workers. This, I feel, is well illustrated by Henry Giarretto, Director of the Child Sexual Abuse Treatment Program, Santa Clara County Juvenile Probation Department, San Jose, California. Addressing a conference on the sexual abuse of children, Giarretto described his first encounter with a family reported for father–daughter incest. The interview with the mother and daughter went well. He was able to listen to their confusion and to share their pain, and they left tearfully relieved. Giarretto then set up an interview with the father, having acquainted himself with the details of the case from the police report. He continued:

> It was a particularly raunchy case: fondling at age five, oral copulation and sodomy at eight, and full vaginal penetration at thirteen. A picture of the panic-stricken face of the girl I had just seen flashed in my brain. Instead of compassion I was wracked by violent feelings toward the offender. I didn't want listen to his side of the story but to kick the bastard in the crotch instead.[1]

In the presentation of their professional sexual selves social workers draw upon their knowledge of human needs, human growth and behaviour, family dynamics and some of the origins of marital breakdown. Their intervention in the sex-related problems of clients or residents is additionally influenced by a number of factors, for instance the expectations of their agency; the extent to which they see themselves as agents of social control; whether they accept and respect the spirit and letter of the laws relating to sexual exchanges, for example concerning the age of consent and the permitted age for homosexual relationships; whether their social work perspective is predominantly psychodynamic or, perhaps, exclusively radical; whether their practice base inclines them towards directive or non-directive interventive techniques; and how their political awareness and sociological knowledge encourage them to question, sometimes more deeply than others, the origins of many of the social ills and social and sexual prejudices with which they are surrounded.

The laws relating to sex

While as a general principle the basis of response in this whole area of social work practice must be 'the recognition of the value and dignity of every human being, irrespective of origin, status, sex, sexual orientation, age, belief or contribution to society',[2] the law is a primary determinant of action. The interpretation of the laws relating to sex and the ways in which they are known to operate will influence social workers' responses to the behaviour of their clients, so for most practitioners their starting point must be what the law says.

The law is apparently quite clear in stating what sexual relationships are permissible.[3] Under section 5 of the Sexual Offences Act (England and Wales) 1956 it is an absolute offence for a man to have intercourse with a girl under 13. Under section 6, it is an offence for a man to have intercourse with a girl between 13 and 16, qualified to the extent that certain defences are available: first, that the man believes himself validly married to the girl (although the marriage itself is not valid); and, secondly, that being under 24 years of age and not previously charged with the same offence, he believes her to be over 16. The maximum penalty for unlawful sexual intercourse with a girl under 16 years of age but over 13 is two years' imprisonment.

The Sexual Offences (Scotland) Act 1976, section 3, prohibits sexual intercourse with a girl under 13 years of age. The maximum penalty could be life imprisonment. Section 4 makes it an offence to have intercourse with a girl between 13 and 16. On indictment the maximum penalty is two years' imprisonment or three months on summary procedure.

The Criminal Law Amendment Act (Northern Ireland) 1885 fixed a maximum penalty of two years' imprisonment for unlawful carnal knowledge of a girl between 14 and 17 years. The age of sexual consent is thus 17, a year older than in the rest of the United Kingdom and presenting an anomalous condition in Northern Ireland where the minimum age for marriage with parental consent is 16 years. An offence against a girl aged under 14 carries a maximum penalty of life imprisonment. There is no defence that the man believed her to be over 17, whatever her age. Although in practice prosecutions are rarely brought in cases where the girl is 16, one such incurred a fine of £200 against a man as recently as March 1978.

Turning to homosexuality, the Sexual Offences Act 1967 provides that sexual acts performed in private between consenting males over the age of 21 years do not constitute a criminal offence in England and Wales. There are, however, special laws forbidding members of the armed forces or merchant seamen from engaging in homosexual relationships. It seems possible that the age limit for homosexual relations between men could be reduced from 21 to 18 years in the near future but this is by no means certain. At present, acts committed with men under 21 years may carry penalties of up to life imprisonment under certain circumstances. In Scotland, until 1980, acts of 'gross indecency' were illegal, carrying a maximum penalty of two years' imprisonment. Since then, however, a change in the law has permitted consenting adults to have homosexual relations, bringing the position into line with England. The maximum penalty in Northern Ireland until 1982 was life imprisonment (in November 1980 the European Court of Human Rights decided that the existing law in Northern Ireland interfered unjustifiably with personal privacy and breached Article 8 of the European Convention).

It is interesting to note that as long ago as 1978 an attempt was made by the then Labour Government to make the law in Northern Ireland the same as in England and Wales. But the Reverend Ian Paisley launched a counter-attack on the Government's discussion paper with a 'Save Ulster from Sodomy' campaign, and a petition against change attracted 70,000 signatures.[4] It was not until 25 October 1982 that an Order bringing the law on homosexuality in Northern Ireland into line with the rest of the United Kingdom was approved in the House of Commons. Members of Parliament were given a free vote and the Order was passed by 168 votes to 21.[5]

In certain European and common law countries where there is a minimum age for homosexual relations, the age varies from 15 to 21. For example, the age is 16 in Holland, Italy and Norway; and 15 in Denmark, Poland and Sweden. A number of countries have the same age for homosexual relations as for heterosexual, and the concept of 'special relationships' is found, among others, in the codes of Norway and Poland.[6] The trend in this country will be examined in Chapter 7.

Incest occurs when there is sexual intercourse between a man and a woman within the prohibited relationships. These are: a man with his daughter, sister or half-sister, mother or granddaughter; and a woman over 16 with her father, brother or half-brother, son or grandfather. Illegitimate children are covered by the law of incest but adopted and step-children are not. The offences relating to unlawful sexual intercourse and indecent assault, however, still apply. Sexual relationships between father and son come within the offences of buggery or indecent assault and not incest or unlawful sexual intercourse.[7] In England and Wales incest by a man carries a maximum sentence of seven years which could be increased to life imprisonment if it occurs with a girl under 13 years of age. The maximum penalty in the case of incest by a woman over 16 is seven years' imprisonment.

Mentally ill and mentally handicapped people are subject to special provisions concerning sexual intercourse.[8] Section 128 of the Mental Health Act 1959 prohibits a male member of staff from having unlawful sexual intercourse (that is, sexual intercourse outside marriage) with a woman who is, for the time being, receiving treatment for mental disorder in the hospital. Although there is no equivalent provision in the case of female staff having intercourse with male patients, it is argued that such behaviour might fall within the remit of section 126 of the 1959 Act which prohibits the ill-treatment of patients.

There is also provision for severely mentally handicapped people who are regarded in law as especially vulnerable to sexual exploitation. Briefly, the law lays down the following prohibitions: that a man may not have illegal (outside marriage) sexual intercourse with a severely mentally handicapped woman (section 7, Sexual Offences Act 1956); that a man may not commit buggery or gross indecency with a severely mentally handicapped man (section 1[3], Sexual Offences Act 1967); that neither a severely mentally handicapped man nor woman can give consent which, for any other person, would prevent any other act from becoming an indecent assault (section 14[4] and section 15[3], Sexual Offences Act 1956); and that a severely mentally handicapped woman may not be procured for the purposes of unlawful sexual intercourse (section 9, Sexual Offences Act 1956).

These laws are, in effect, designed to prohibit severely mentally handicapped people from having sexual relationships outside marriage. On a strict interpretation of the law many feel that they work against the liberalisation of attitudes to sexual relations between handicapped people, liberalisation more than ever apparent in some residential settings.

Changing values

Set out boldly in this way the law seems singularly out of touch with many of the sexual activities and sexual attitudes of today. But deviants are treated according to the formal and informal laws of the moment. In matters of sexuality these have shown considerable variation over the years and, I would suggest, are at present in turmoil. As we have seen, the laws are even different in different parts of the United Kingdom. Who can tell what will be acceptable or unacceptable in 20 years' time or at the end of the decade? I would agree that the protective functions of the law play an essential role in sexual relationships between people of unequal power. This is well argued, for example, by Anthony Storr in his consideration of incestuous relationships[9] and few would dispute the need for the support of a legal framework. Nevertheless, there are many incidents in social work practice which are questionable regarding their classification as 'offences'. In too many instances society – through its representatives – pounces, punishes and conveys guilt with alacrity, barely pausing to examine the often infinite implications of its actions.

This question is made even more complex because of the way in which relative power between people is affected not only by age and gender but by class and employment. The apparently weaker partner is not always at a disadvantage in power relationships and many examples underline this ambiguity. The issue has to be examined case by case. Why are we so much more bothered by power differences in matters of sex – which are not perhaps so easy to define as the law would have us believe – than, say, in matters of education, work or punishment? In the minds of some people the 'immorality' arising from an imbalance of power in these other aspects of our societal structure merits far greater outcry and condemnation.

However, the concepts of 'unequal power base' and 'assault on the person' may, in fact, be the fundamental ideas to be enshrined in any revision of the laws about sex. In a changing society these two principles may lead towards a far healthier approach and avoid what, on standing back, I perceive in many instances as an absolute nonsense. How can we permit a 17-year-old youth to be labelled a criminal because he has had a sexual relationship with a 15-year-old girl with her consent, particularly when such relationships happen daily and attract no comment? How is it possible to punish a young man of 22 years who, as a result of friendship and affection, has a sexual relationship with his 17-year-old male friend? Technically these are offences and people still occasionally find themselves in court for them, may even be put on probation as a result and become clients of social workers. The ages are arbitrary and the offences are man-made – as if seeking to protect earlier codes of conduct that probably never existed.

Assessing relative power may, of course, be more difficult when in the case of a 15-year-old girl the man is 27, 37, 47 or even 57; and in the case of the 17-year-old youth when the man is 32, 42 or 52. As the law stands, punishment is quite crudely based on age difference alone, and often determined by some notion of an 'acceptable age gap' in the minds of a few people responsible for framing and administering the law, and reflecting what they feel are public moral standards. There may be other criteria to be used in arguments for and against punishment, and Peter Righton makes the point that 'chronological age by itself is both arbitrary and misleading as an indication of a person's need to be "protected" from adult sexual advances'.[10]

Elsewhere I have described the relationship between 15-year-old Dawn, a girl in care, and 52-year-old Syd.[11] They eventually lived together for four years after 18 months of very affectionate courtship and constant battles against 'authority'. The relationship was a mutually satisfying one, although from the start the 'power' rested firmly with Dawn. At the beginning there were those who would have preferred to have had Syd 'frightened off' on the basis of the age difference and the supposedly unequal power base in his favour. With hindsight this would have denied Dawn what I later realised even more strongly was a relationship with Syd which was the vehicle for personal growth and a great deal of happiness.

While the law may wish to appear sure in what it will allow – although we know in practice that there are significant differences both in prosecutions for the same offence and in sentencing policy – there are now few codes in the commercial world from which young or old can seek guidance. Despite legislation, almost anything is acceptable. The codes that do remain are mostly traditional, religious and family based, relying heavily on guilt, the virtue of delayed gratification, a denial of adolescent sexuality and a comparatively old-fashioned view of the sanctity of the marriage bed for their continuation. These are now far less important to many people, totally rejected by others, not sustained by the thousands who divorce each year and do not form part of the experience of many among the growing number of unmarried mothers. Many would see this as a time of re-evaluation, the moment of history when it may be possible to make some shift in sexual values, enabling people to enjoy new levels of sexual satisfaction while reducing the pathological component of sex which so many clients and residents are caught up in.

I mean no disrespect to those who hold dear traditional values, and have no wish to erode their freedom of choice, but am concerned about other people, young and not so young, tethered and tortured by sets of rules which they see as irrationally perpetuated in the very different social and sexual climate of the 1980s.

A few months ago I was working with a group of young people in a community home and noticed that one of the girls, Sammy – a few days before her fifteenth birthday – was engrossed in a paperback by Scott Spencer, *Endless Love*. As I had just finished the same novel – having been enticed to buy it after reading the first chapter in a transatlantic in-flight magazine – the book was a natural topic of conversation. Sammy was eager to discuss the story, a well-written tale of teenage love and passion recommended for all who work intensively in the field of feelings and emotions. As an integral part of the story it contains two main explicitly sexual passages, the first of which reads:

Once when Jade and I were making love in her bedroom, around the time when we first got the double bed, and we'd been making love for so long that she was as wet as a river inside and could hardly feel me anymore and I could hardly feel her but we needed, for reasons that really weren't physical, to keep on making love, she turned over on her belly and raised herself on her knees. I thought she was asking me to come in from behind, where the tilt of the vagina gives the illusion of newness and tightness, as we had done so many times. Her back was soaked with sweat and the sheets were like slush. I was panting and sweating myself and sore all over but I didn't want to stop, neither of us did. The friction, our need of it, wasn't really connected to pleasure at that point. It was more of an attempt to *erase* our bodies and explode out of them into pure matter. It was afternoon, there was soft light in her little room, and when she spread her legs and offered her rump to me I looked at the back half of her vagina, with the dark brown hair sopping wet and poking out in curly spikes . . . at once I began to move myself into her. But she stopped me and said something a little bewildering, like Put it in the other one, something uncharacteristically peek-a-booish like that, but which I completely understood. I didn't want to say no but I was immediately nervous. We'd never done that before and I didn't want to leave her alone in her willingness to go somewhere new . . . I thought you'd like it, she said. No, I don't think I would, I said. My stomach was pounding like a second heart. I stretched out beside her, with my leg resting on her thighs and my arms around her. It would be all right, Jade said. Because it's you and me and we love each other. I wanted to do it because neither of us have ever done it before. It would be ours.[12]

For Sammy the book was serious and compulsive reading. She sought my reaction to it, and to the sexually descriptive passages. I doubt whether the staff of the home knew exactly what the book contained although I later discovered that one of them had read it. An emotionally powerful tale, it was, I consider, much better reading for Sammy than the violent sexual material which falls into the hands of young people and is surreptitiously read under the bedclothes or in the school toilets. And I told her so.

Better, too, than an excess of the often clinical sex education pamphlets showing illustrations of an assortment of flaccid and erect penises, lifeless vaginas, tubes of contraceptive jelly, curiously-shaped condoms and intra-uterine devices. I saw *Endless Love* as a most appropriate book to follow the excellent publication by Jane Cousins, *Make it Happy*,[13] a copy of which I knew Sammy already had in her possession. Sammy said she had been recommended *Endless Love* by her English teacher. She had mentioned it to her social worker who did not know the book, but wanted to borrow it when Sammy had finished reading it.

Sammy herself was on the verge of engaging in a sexual relationship. She was preparing herself for it. She needed to do so without guilt; with understanding; with knowledge and without fear of the boundaries of intimate physical exchanges with a male; and, above all, with an awareness of the intensity of the feelings which could legitimately stir within her. *Endless Love* is a story in which sex is a natural consequence of the relationship between Jade Butterfield and David Axelrod. The sexual act is depicted as *mutually* exciting, rewarding and satisfying, but non-violent, aspects of a relationship not always appreciated by young people, and especially young people growing up in care.

Sammy had lived in a community home for a number of years. She had learned about sex from her friends and from the limited sex education programme in the denominational secondary school she attended. Until the recent arrival of the new head of home sex had been regarded as nasty and dirty by most of the children and young people she lived with. But there had been changes – even though many of the staff found difficulty in acknowledging the children and young people as healthy sexual beings – and Sammy was exercising her right to obtain whatever help she needed in preparation for an adult sexual life. She told me that she had never understood how so much violence could be associated with sex which, from her reading, and obvious exploratory sex play, she saw as 'quite beautiful'.

Sammy was making her own preparations and used discussion with sympathetic adults to alleviate any anxieties. I would suggest, however, that many other young people with whom we work, boys especially, lack Sammy's potential for self-education, and need appropriate reading and frank discussion in order to overcome their fears and to reverse the decidedly unhealthy – and sometimes brutal – attitudes to sex which they absorb from pornographic magazines and the media. And young people do obtain without difficulty considerable quantities of 'hard porn'. Last year I saw the walls of a 15-year-old boy's bedroom in a closed unit covered with the most evil pictures of sexual violence, sickening in their portrayal of the sexual act.

I was therefore pleased to see Sammy reading *Endless Love*, and have every confidence that she will move into young adulthood a sexually mature person, capable of strong, comforting and mutually satisfying relationships. For those less fortunate and more disturbed than Sammy, like the boy in secure accommodation, every effort must be made by social workers, among others, to give them similar chances of eventually finding fulfilment through their sexual selves.

I can understand the apprehension – and even anger – of those adults for whom some passages in *Endless Love* would be an anathema. Ten years ago, on finding such a book in the hands of an adolescent, I would have undoubtedly reacted in a different manner. Nowadays I feel that the only hope of reversing the destructive and extremely 'sick' attitudes towards sex and its close links with the worst possible types of violence is – to draw on part of a quotation used in Chapter 2 – to ensure 'that such an activity becomes a positive and constructive experience in the developmental process leading to responsible adulthood.'[14]

The extract from *Endless Love* is among the 'milder' material that some young people have access to. If this is the sort of literature that adults make freely available – and they do – and if this is the literature that some young people are reading, then there is a responsibility to work with the consequences. Furthermore, in a full and healthy sexual exchange – which Sammy may be engaged in and enjoying within a very short space of time – her experience, if adults are honest about their own relationships, may be as explosive as Jade's and David's. Unprepared, she could be overwhelmed – with all that that entails.

The range of problems
In making an analysis of the sex-related problems of clients and residents the following would be among the main difficulties to be found: inadequate or incomplete sex education; misunderstanding of sexual signals and appropriate sexual responses within social relationships; an upbringing which presented sex as nasty and dirty; ideas within women that sex is something done to females by males

and not a totally mutual experience; ideas within men of sexual intercourse as a far more aggressive act than it need be, and one to which women submit; frustration resulting from the lack of opportunity for sexual expression, sometimes engendered by the very establishments we expect people to live in; and, above all, deeply-seated guilt extending, in its extreme, to the still-present six-in-the-marriage-bed fantasy – a constantly handicapping feature of too many potentially comforting sexual relationships.

The sexual values and the attitudes to sex laid down in childhood and adolescence do undoubtedly have an effect on a person's future social and sexual relationships. Unhappy sexual experiences in adult life may well have their origins in particular incidents or as the result of an accumulation of influences during earlier years. For some people one bitter sexual experience on top of another throughout their lives may sooner or later permeate their whole beings, making them sexually suspicious, sexually withdrawn and sexually handicapped. They may endeavour to build an asexual wall around themselves, a wall constantly assailed by what their bodies keep telling them through series of mixed messages, by the physical sensations they experience, by the moments when they themselves break through their own wall of asexuality and by the sexual morse code which informs and determines vast areas of human conduct, and social and working relationships. For other people, moving through life's ages and stages, steadily increasing comfort with themselves as sexual beings brings about a generosity of spirit and a bodily self-satisfaction that find their expression not only in a sexual relationship – or sexual relationships – but in other aspects of their character and their behaviour.

Because of the rather clumsy ways in which children and young people are introduced to and taught how to manage their sexuality, most people are at some point between the two extremes I have described. Social workers may find that some of those who become their clients will have experienced, or are experiencing, their sexuality as a destructive force. Sometimes this is only a temporary setback. The client may make the issue explicit, it may already have been made explicit because of the nature of the referral or the social worker may pick it up in the context of other problems. On other occasions, the sexual handicap is so great – or may appear so chronic – that it has to become the principal focus of the work with the client. Without intensive work he or she may be permanently less able to operate with success in other spheres of life. The case study on pp. 36–8 illustrates this well.

In working with children and young people; in responding to referrals throughout the age span on the basis of scant knowledge but which may cloak any type of problem; and in helping those who – on their own admission or because of a sexual difficulty that has brought them into conflict with the law or society's values – have massive, unresolved sexual uncertainties and dilemmas, social workers may at any time be called upon to make sense of and to intervene with purpose in this most sensitive area. They can only do this with credibility from a worked-out philosophy and a thought-out value base at least as good as those of 'average man'. With training, insight, experience and the special personal qualities which they bring to the job it is expected that their contribution will be much greater.

This book is written with that end in mind. It makes suggestions about responding more confidently to the sexuality of young people; it identifies the alienation that may occur when sexual relationships go wrong; it asks social workers to consider the effects of residential care on the sex lives of residents; it invites them to think more positively about the sexual needs of handicapped people; it asks for more enlightened responses to sexual abuse, especially in regard to the ever-hasty and often totally destructive labelling of 'victims' and 'offenders' – words used in this text, but often with strong reservations; and it makes a plea for more professional and more humane ways of inquiring into allegations in residential establishments.

There is a great deal yet to be understood, yet to be done in respect of sex and the social worker. It is an exciting field of work – and we should not be afraid of acknowledging this – and a rewarding area of practice because, striking as it does at the very centre of human behaviour and human motivation, it embraces with an intensity nowhere else experienced to the same degree the heights and depths of feelings and emotions.

2 Sex and Young People

The age at which young people become sexually active is falling and in many day schools efforts are made within the sex education programme of the social education course to respond to this. Young people in some parts of the country talk freely in mixed classes about reproduction, contraception, masturbation and venereal diseases, although some local authorities still insist that the topic of homosexuality should not be broached unless first raised by the pupils.[1] Perhaps it should also be acknowledged that some adults, at least, hope that if youngsters talk about sex they are less likely to try it.

In any discussion about the sexual relationships of young people I take as my base line the report of a working party of the World Health Organization on young people aged 14 to 18 years:

> While induced abortion may be better than an unwanted child, contraception is better than an unwanted pregnancy and the best path to improved contraception is education for responsible sexual behaviour. Increasing sexual activity among teenagers is a fact and, rather than ignoring its existence or trying to stamp it out, it would seem more expedient to educate young people so that such an activity becomes a positive and constructive experience in the developmental process leading to responsible adulthood.[2]

A major survey of 14-year-old Danish pupils carried out in 1976 showed that, of those questioned, 16 per cent of boys and 13 per cent of girls had had sexual intercourse.[3] In the United Kingdom it is known that nearly a quarter of 15-year-olds regularly engage in genital apposition and about 10 per cent have sexual intercourse,[4] and a more recent study, again in this country, indicates that one girl in eight has sexual intercourse before she is 16, a total of 40,000 a year.[5]

Some would suggest that the percentage figures for young people who become clients of social workers are higher. Certainly, many adolescents on supervision orders or on care orders are sexually active. While young people of 14 and 15 years do experiment and may be at risk of pregnancy some find considerable satisfaction and comfort in a sexual relationship. It must be remembered that: 'for the majority of the human race, self-esteem is chiefly rooted in sexuality . . . the object of physical passion is thus not only a means whereby the drive of sexuality can be expressed and assuaged, but is also a vital source of self-esteem.'[6] Many young clients are especially low in self-esteem. In matters of bodily attraction and sexual performance they may feel, at least temporarily, able to regain some of the self-esteem lost in other areas of their lives, for example, in social and educational performance.

As further illustrated in Chapter 6, some young people are well aware of their sexual power and how to use it to their advantage. Dave, an education welfare officer, was asked by his senior colleague to call at 15-year-old Sandy's house. She had only attended school on two occasions during the autumn term and it was mid-November. Reports on file show that there had never been any serious problems before about Sandy's attendance at secondary school although, as her mother was frequently away from home, it was suspected that her boyfriend had moved in. One note on the file labelled her as 'promiscuous'. Dave called at the house, Sandy was in and he spoke to her about her attendance. She was clearly not interested in returning to school but saw her way out of the dilemma. 'Let's go to bed', she said, 'and forget about school.' Dave neither took up the suggestion nor prolonged the interview, taking the first opportunity to leave the house although he did admit, in talking about his experience, to finding Sandy an attractive girl. He could not share the incident with his supervisor, fearing ridicule or veiled messages about having given Sandy the 'come on'. So nothing was said and Dave never went to the house again. Not for the first, nor probably the last, time had Sandy experienced her sexuality as powerful.

The age of consent

The body mechanism does not respond to an arbitrary 'age of consent' of 16 years in its need for sexual activity. Significantly, in many other European and common law countries, a lower age is fixed. Subject to special relationship provisions, the normal age of consent is 14 in Austria, Germany and Yugoslavia; and 15 in Denmark, France, Poland and Sweden. As far as it is possible to generalise, the trend in certain European countries seems to be towards lowering the age.[7] In view of the evidence that young people under 16 are able to enjoy sexual relationships, some adults find difficulty in reconciling the current age of consent in this country and certain sections of the Sexual Offences Act 1956 with the falling age of puberty. As suggested earlier, a healthy sexual relationship in adolescence may, in the long term, be better for mental health than an adolescence spent furtively exploring pornographic magazines and bearing the guilt imposed by the taboos of adults caught up in the tentacles of an outwardly prudish Victorian era.

The young need protection against 'exploitation' no less than any other vulnerable group but, as in all areas of social work practice, we must be prepared to think and act laterally when the inevitable event occurs. In any case, what is exploitation? Who has the right – who should have the right? – to decide what is exploitative and what is not? The law as it stands is not necessarily helpful in this respect and the arguments in favour of the repeal of the age of consent contained in the report *Pregnant at School* – referred to later in the chapter – are especially valuable in this debate.[8]

If a sexual relationship does happen in the life of a 15-year-old the task of the social worker, field or residential, does not lie in making the young person feel guilty and of low esteem – yet again – thereby increasing the need for secrecy. It seems preferable to help him or her to understand it, not to feel anxious about it, to control it and – most often – to enjoy it. The adult attitudes of disapproval and censure together with the imposition of obstacles and unreasonable restrictions leading to scenes of confrontation, alienation and despair are never constructive, especially in the face of the agonising searches made by many young people as they strive to 'belong'. Helping the adolescent to manage a relationship within the boundaries he or she desires would appear to be a better approach. Adult fears of promiscuity are usually ill founded, 'promiscuity' being an adult definition of behaviour – quite a nasty definition, I feel – and one which many young people would not agree with.

I am aware that 'the development of an individual's sexuality is a long and complicated process involving the interaction among biological, psychological and social factors'[9] and that there is often a gap between psychological and biological development. In filling this gap, however, the social worker has to ensure that he or she does not give the negative messages likely to widen it but, more fruitfully, provides understanding as sexual relationships emerge.

Contraception under 16

Under the Family Law Reform Act 1969 16-year-olds have a right to consent to their own medical treatment without parental knowledge, and this includes advice and practical assistance in matters of contraception. Hopefully, the exercise of this right is given active support by those working with older adolescents. For those under 16 a preventive service is also available, but the decision whether or not to prescribe contraception for a younger girl rests with the clinical judgement of a doctor. The original DHSS Family Planning Service Memorandum of Guidance, May 1974, section G (issued with HSC[15]32), stated that advice on the doctor's legal position in prescribing contraception was that 'he is not acting unlawfully provided he acts in good faith in protecting the girl against the potentially harmful effects of intercourse'. The Medical Defence Union advised that the doctor should not contact parents without the patient's permission, but that it would be prudent for the doctor to seek the patient's consent to tell the parents. The girl's refusal to give permission could, it was stated, affect the nature of the advice given.

In December 1980 the DHSS reissued section G of the Family Planning Service Memorandum of Guidance to stress that the DHSS would hope that the doctor 'will always seek to persuade the child to involve the parent or guardian' but reiterated that, in the final analysis, the decision whether or not to prescribe contraception must be for the clinical judgement of a doctor. Not unnaturally, some adults hold strong opinions about the wisdom of supplying contraceptives to young people under 16 years of age. The following, under the headline 'Crack down on GPs over Pill kids', is representative of comments being made at the time in the popular press:

> Doctors should be prosecuted for not telling parents when a schoolgirl asks to go on to the Pill, a GP claimed yesterday. For they are encouraging under-age sex, said Dr Adrian Rogers . . . 'They actually think they are being clever and wise . . . If a child is having intercourse and requesting contraception the doctor should inform the legal guardians and hope they have the good sense to prosecute the man involved. A parent discovering a child on the Pill, prescribed by a doctor, should not only have recourse in a criminal court to the man abusing his child – but also to the doctor for conspiring in the behaviour.'[10]

Undoubtedly social workers are confronted with questions of morality in their work with sexually active and potentially active young people. The advice they give, the attitudes they convey, must be based on what appears, professionally, to be in the best interests of the individuals involved but, as we have seen in Chapter 1, it is not always easy to separate our personal and our professional sexual selves. However, both the Memorandum of Guidance issued in

1974 and that which appeared in 1980 extend the protection given to doctors to other professional workers, section G now reading:

> The Department would therefore hope that in any case where a doctor or other professional worker is approached by a person under the age of 16 for advice in these matters, the doctor, or other professional, will always seek to persuade the child to involve the parent or guardian (or other person in loco parentis) at the earliest stage of consultation, and will proceed from the assumption that it would be most unusual to provide advice about contraception without parental consent.
>
>   It is, however, widely accepted that consultations between doctors and patients are confidential; and the Department recognises the importance which doctors and patients attach to this principle. It is a principle which applies also to other professions concerned. To abandon this principle for children under 16 might cause some not to seek professional advice at all . . . The Department realises that in such exceptional cases the nature of any counselling must be a matter for the doctor or any other professional worker concerned and that the decision whether or not to prescribe contraception must be for the clinical judgement of the doctor.

A further statement is made in *The Handbook of Medical Ethics*, issued by the British Medical Association in 1981. This says that when a doctor is unable to obtain the patient's consent to involve parents he must decide 'whether the girl has the mental maturity to understand the possible consequences of her action. If she has not, then her consent is not informed and so invalid. If he is satisfied that she can consent, he makes a clinical decision as to whether the provision of contraception is in the best interests of the patient' (p. 18).

It is important to note that, once again, the laws in Scotland and Northern Ireland are slightly different. The Family Law Reform Act does not cover Scotland which, of course, has a different legal system and different legislation on many issues. The relevant act is the Age of Majority Act 1969. Although like its English equivalent it reduces the age of majority for voting to 18 it is silent on the matter of consent to medical, surgical and dental treatment. However, both Acts were based on the same Latey Commission which recommended medical consent at 16 so it is practice in Scotland, based also on common law, to allow a 16-year-old to give consent.

The DHSS Memorandum of Guidance 1974 was restricted to England and Wales, and the Scottish Home and Health Department issued its own circular on 28 March 1974: NHS Circular (Gen)

5. This made no mention of the under-16s in discussion of the new family planning service, nor is there guidance of the sort given by the Medical Defence Union in the DHSS circular. However, in the second paragraph the position of the unmarried is made quite clear: 'The family planning services shall therefore be available to all who need them and . . . should be so organised as to avoid any bar to the provision of services to the unmarried.' Therefore, as in England and Wales, a doctor must use his or her clinical judgement in the case of minors, but confidentiality is seen as the right of every patient.

As stated in Chapter 1, the age of consent is 17 in Northern Ireland, one year higher than in the rest of the United Kingdom. With the age of majority 18 and the medical age of consent 16, family planning clinics will deal with anyone of 16 and over, regardless of marital status or sex. While the position regarding young people under 16 is the same as in England and Wales – doctors must use clinical judgement about giving treatment but should not breach their patient's confidence – it seems less likely that a girl under 16 would be prescribed contraceptives without her parents' consent.

Changing attitudes

Despite the official shift of emphasis between 1974 and 1980 in England and Wales, other indications are that a more liberal policy is emerging. Two important reports appeared in 1979, one representing professional opinion (*Pregnant at School*),[11] and the other – although unequivocal in its stance that the age of consent should be retained at 16 – presenting facts that, in reality, ran counter to its recommendations.[12] The first report suggested that as adequate protection for minors is provided by other existing legislation, the law relating to the age of consent should be repealed. It concluded:

> We argue that the law is out of touch with current behaviour because it does not take account of consensual sexual relationships among the young and therefore unjustly penalises the boys . . . The practice of many professionals – judges, general practitioners, police, social workers – reflects the view that the law is inappropriate in today's sexual climate. (p. 52)

The second report, the work of the Policy Advisory Committee on Sexual Offences, although advocating no change in the law, acknowledged that:

. . . comparatively few cases of unlawful sexual intercourse with girls under 16 known to the police end in prosections; for example, in 1977 although 3681 such offences were known to the police and 3433 were described as cleared up, only 558 persons were prosecuted.[13]

Many sexual relationships between young people, including relationships in which one or both partners may be under 16 years of age, develop from mutual concern and affection. I have been struck recently by the very large number of couples I know – those in their twenties as well as those in their sixties – who first met and enjoyed a close relationship when they were 14 or 15 years of age. Heavy-handed intervention – in the absence of violence or 'exploitation' – carries with it an awesome responsibility whatever adults may feel about one or both of the young people. Whenever possible, society's response should be supportive and not destructive.

Social workers do need to think carefully about the advice they give, and about their responsibilities *vis-à-vis* both boys and girls. For example, we know that oral contraceptives present special problems for some adolescents. As the biological maturation process is probably not complete until two or three years after menarche and since there is lack of knowledge about the effects of hormonal contraception during maturation, girls who are sexually active and wish to avoid pregnancy during the early adolescent period are recommended to use non-steroidal contraceptives.[14] Although the pill is by far the most commonly used method of contraception – and the one causing the most frequent health scares – it is for many adults the easiest to discuss and the one most distanced from the act of sexual intercourse. And even social workers can feel uncomfortable about talking to young people about sex, either not wanting to appear to enjoy such discussion 'too much' or by being so clinical that they bore or mystify those in need of counsel or factual information. However, it is only right to consider alternatives to oral contraceptives and, further, to work with boys too in discussing their responsibilities. I suspect that this is still all too rarely done with adolescent boys – particularly in residential care – and that too many engage in sexual activity without adequate information about contraception, later regretting the pregnancies of their girlfriends. Indeed, for those living away from home such curriculum developments as those mentioned at the beginning of the chapter must, first, be extended within residential settings to take account of the additional intimacies of group living; and, secondly, in establishments with education on the premises, we must ensure that a comparable programme of sex education is presented together with discussion and sexual counselling suited to the special needs of those wrestling with emotional and social problems.

A recent case gave me cause for concern. Five girls in the fifth form of a comprehensive school became pregnant during the academic year 1980–81. When the pregnancies were confirmed two girls were 16, the others 15. All had conceived when 14 or 15 years of age. The four girls living with their parents decided to have their babies, and to keep them. Two subsequently returned to school. The fifth girl lived in a community home and very soon had an abortion. The decision was made within days. Counselling took the form of persuasion, within the context of a power relationship. Her boyfriend was not consulted and the girl was loaded with guilt and shame. The guilt, I feel, should rightfully have belonged to the adults who cared for her. They failed to ensure that she was given adequate advice about contraception and could not acknowledge the sexual side of her relationship with her boyfriend, a rewarding human experience in which both found love and security. Neither could they consider allowing her to keep her baby.

Residential care
Again, the following example presents a not uncommon challenge to many residential staff:

> One of the girls in an adolescent hostel, Jane, is found to be pregnant. She has already had her fifteenth birthday. Since admission 18 months previously Jane has maintained a balanced and affectionate relationship with Michael, another resident who is a year older than Jane. She admits that Michael is the father of her unborn child.

Which establishment would now be able to contain both the boy and the girl? Which would be forced to recommend transfer, then dampen the conversations of those remaining, many of whom would have been 'in the know'? Can we *really* legislate for the expression of sexuality in the case of these two young people? It is interesting that few unmarried adolescent mothers feel 'sinful' and 'different' until made to experience this by the comments and attitudes of those who surround them.[15] The primary question must be: How can we best help Jane and Michael? All else is secondary. The 'neatest' solution – abortion or transfer or 'punishment', for example, by separation – has proved time and time again to be the most damaging. Occasionally it is possible to find day nursery accommodation so that unmarried schoolgirl mothers who live with their parents, friends or relatives can continue their education. The difference between them and their friends at school is thus minimised, and large areas of normal, everyday functioning are preserved. Should we provide less, should we stigmatize more, merely on the grounds that a girl is living in a residential centre under the care of a local authority or voluntary organisation? Because he fathered a child in his 14-year-old girlfriend would Michael have been sent away from home had he been living with his parents?

Residential care is often experienced as restrictive by many adolescents. It is not difficult to increase these feelings if the advice and practical help – for example, about contraception – available to their peers of 14 or 15 living in their own homes is not made available to young people in care. Some members of social services committees, and certainly some managers of voluntary bodies, find it necessary to oppose contraception for girls under 16. Such an attitude needs to be taken up in discussion by senior officers of departments and with voluntary organisations in a way that indicates support for those working closely with teenagers in residential homes.

There are, however, social workers who work purposefully in a different way while respecting confidentiality in personal matters. A young member of staff, Pamela, told me that she was purchasing condoms for two of the 15-year-old boys in the voluntary community home where she worked as a group leader, 'because they are too embarrassed to buy them themselves'. She had not been able to share what she was doing with the head of home or any other members of staff and feared their reaction. Pamela was extremely concerned about developing sexually responsible attitudes in the boys in her care, but was aware of her delicate position if the managers of the home learned of her actions. Her method of working with those in her care had no place in the philosophy of that particular home.

The continuing debate about sex in residential establishments seems likely to remain especially heated in respect of living and working with young people, but as case law is built up with one client group its effect will be felt by those working in other residential settings. Ways of meeting the needs of adults living away from their own homes will be considered later. This chapter dwells particularly on children and adolescents; on the sexual needs and rights of young people; and on some aspects of the sexually-based exchanges arising between adults and young people. Further changes in attitude and developments in practice will continue to call for skill, compassion, tolerance and sensitivity of a high order.

The importance of touch

Before moving on to illustrate appropriate and inappropriate approaches to the sexuality of young residents I would like to reflect on a related area of human conduct central to the quality of life of many people: touch. Living in a world wherein all owe their very existence to touch in reproduction and early mothering it has relevance for social work with a range of clients, is especially important when working with people in residential settings and has a crucial part to play in the upbringing of children and young people. It is for this reason that the topic has been included in this chapter.

Most people have a need for close human contact which involves touching and stroking. Berne suggests that: 'Of all the forms of sensation the one preferred by most human beings is contact with another human skin. This provides not only touch, but also warmth or heat of a special kind.'[16] Such contact, it is said, may make the difference between physical and mental health or breakdown. The taboo on touch remains strong in many residential centres while the need for close physical contact is compounded by the isolation – either occasional or permanent – experienced by many people, young and old, in group living.

Suttie makes reference to the taboo on tenderness. His thesis that modern science has a positive aversion to anything savouring of sentimentality[17] has double implications for those living in residential establishments. Not only are they subject to the pressures of 'modern science' but are sometimes cared for by staff who themselves feel uneasy about close physical contact, either with residents or other people, thus accentuating the taboo.

In deprecating current approaches which fail to allow children time to outgrow their childishness, Suttie considers the defences which are hastily built against painful loss:

As I see it, this protective indifference is essentially a 'sour grapes' kind of self-comfort – a self-insulation from love hunger by the 'cultivation' of a 'loveshyness' – but it *demands a psychic blindness to pathos of any kind* – a refusal to participate in emotion. It can be carried to such a point that the individual is not only 'steeled against' the appeal and suffering of others, but he actually dreads appealing to their sympathy, and may, for example, conceal illness for fear of making a 'fuss' or 'scene'. One can only suppose that the privation of love is here recognized as so inevitable, yet the longing remains so painful, that the whole conflict is forced out of mind. Anything that tends to arouse it (pathos and sentiment) is therefore resented exactly as the prude resents an erotic suggestion and for the same reason. The taboo upon regressive longings extends to all manifestations of affection until we can neither offer nor tolerate affection.[18]

Suttie draws attention to unconscious love hunger as a motive for the 'flight into illness', to the widespread incidence of 'disease' of this origin and to the later substitution of sex for love. He further comments that 'The undefended, unreserved character makes a far better parent' (p. 75). How many such young men and young women emerge from residential care?

Young people have a nervous system crying out for physical sensation. In *The Prodigy* Hesse describes the growing relationship between Hans Giebenrath and Hermann Heilner, two boys under stress in a boarding school:

They looked at each other. It was probably the first time they had ever studied each other's face and felt that behind each other's smooth features lived an individual person, a kindred spirit, with his own peculiarities.

Slowly Hermann Heilner stretched out his arm, gripped Hans by the shoulder and drew him towards himself until their cheeks were quite close. Then Hans in a sudden exquisite panic felt his friend's lips touch his own.[19]

There are many contacts involving touch which are acceptable in residential work: bathing children, tending the sick and injured of all ages, comforting in distress, restraining in anger and responding to some of the demands for affection. In most of these the initiative stems from the social worker and only in the latter instance, when responding to the demands of a child, does it usually originate from the resident. For some, of course, what constitutes 'response' and what is meant by 'children' are searching questions. Staff members, too, have touch needs. Skin contact with residents may, consciously or unconsciously, satisfy their own longings. And the physical make-up of many young children – their size, their skin texture and their openness of expression – provides a massive invitation to intimacy. The onlooker, therefore, whether resident or staff member, may well interpret 'response' as 'initiation' and in some establishments physical contact is limited to the very young. In others, however, the climate allows for touch between staff and even older adolescents as part of their developmental and compensatory needs.

Is it possible to divorce touch from sexuality? Sometimes what is sexually significant for the resident holds no such meaning for the worker. Alternatively, a sexually significant act for the latter may be unregistered by the resident. Rarely, I would maintain, is the exchange without sexual meaning for either party, but this does not of necessity make it 'dangerous' or offer immediate grounds for 'suspicion'.

In an important section on physical communication with children Trieschman and his colleagues consider particularly: (i) physical contact and peer group rivalry; (ii) physical contact and sexual stimulation; (iii) physical contact as an anxiety-producing stimulus; and (iv) physical contact and aggression.[20] Jealousy and competition among children for physical contact often result in strong feelings being displayed. The origins of some allegations made against adults have as their roots uncontrollable upsurges of rivalry resulting from seeming rejection or lack of attention from a favoured member of staff. Many children are sexually stimulated by physical contact. The dividing line is thin between those children for whom 'holding' in a temper tantrum is comforting and secure and those for whom it is sexually arousing. Perhaps it is not even possible to make such a distinction. Staff needs at this time must not be forgotten and events can easily slide into a mutually seductive process. On the other hand, as Trieschman points out, some children will misinterpret even the most innocuous contact as a sexual advance, basing their fears on earlier experiences of assault or brutality. The introduction of tenderness to the lives of such children is electrically charged but remains a principal task in working towards their ability to relate and to communicate. As regards aggression, it is often possible to observe over-reaction in the everyday staff–child rough and tumble. Again, in restraining a child – either in play or in a temper tantrum – prolonged holding by a member of staff may produce unnecessary mutual aggression, not only during the particular incident, but later continued as part of the longer-term struggle for dominance.

In working with young people in residential establishments there does seem a particularly fine interplay between sexuality and aggression. As Storr remarks, we know little about the biochemical states underlying tension but:

One interesting fact is that the state of the body in sexual arousal and in aggressive arousal is extremely similar. Kinsey lists fourteen physiological changes which are common to both sexual arousal and anger, and in fact can only discover four physiological changes which are different in the two states of emotion.[21]

The high levels of aggression – not necessarily 'fighting' – in many residential homes and schools are only marginally lowered by the traditional efforts directed towards diversion and sublimation. Downes maintains that the fall in the age of marriage – and to this we could perhaps add increased sexual activity among young people – has done more to keep delinquency rates down than all the intervention we so relentlessly employ.[22]

It helps, I feel, to be clear that the responses discussed above are natural and usually healthy. They are normal and human but are intensified by the close living and the intimate interaction of those concerned. They become unhealthy when the climate of the establishment is such that the feelings which are aroused can only be diverted underground and act as a springboard for later violent eruption. Without a climate in which feelings can be expressed and explored, both in individual and group supervisory sessions, there are few residential centres which exist long without hurt to a resident or a staff member following some issue of overwhelming emotions in which touch, sexuality, jealousy and anger become enmeshed. Later discussion about victims and offenders will illustrate this further.

The taboo on touch in some residential establishments acts strongly against what is regarded by some as developmental need. As Pease says, 'The story of the loss of this important channel of communication as a child gets older is one of the great untold stories of child psychology.'[23] In much the same way as sex itself, touch has untapped potential as a comforting agent and a communication process. Its denial must impoverish further the lives of many people both in their own homes and in residential settings. As a friend of mine, Elinor Goldschmied, has so aptly said, 'Touch is also a language.'

Working with staff and residents
Two distinguishing features of community homes working towards the completion of their transition from approved schools or from the more formal children's home approach of an earlier period – and there are still many examples of both in our midst – are: first, the quality of communication existing between the adults and the

young people, and among the adults themselves; and, secondly, the opportunities available through staff meetings, small group discussions, individual supervision and consultancy for the exploration of incidents arising from the intimacies of daily living. Incidents of a sexual nature are appropriately brought to such meetings. Where there is no vehicle for discussion the individual is left to manage his or her feelings in the best way possible.

The following experiences of three female students, a newly-qualified female member of staff and a recently-appointed, unqualified male member of staff, all in their twenties, illustrate typical exchanges.

Joy was initially taken aback by the behaviour of Alan, a slightly retarded but affectionate 13-year-old. Each night, when Joy was putting him to bed, he would fondle her breasts. She decided not to prevent him and used the occasion to give Alan a cuddle. This diverted him, did not make him feel rejected and was, in Joy's opinion, the way to return his affection. But the contact worried her. She found Alan an attractive boy and warmed to his embrace. After a week or so the security of the unit staff meeting allowed Joy to express her anxiety. She found that two other young females, members of the permanent staff, were having similar experiences and they evolved a joint plan which allowed Alan to continue while they talked to him about more conventional ways for a young person to show his affection. Gradually Alan responded.

Tina's concern was also at bedtime, in a room shared by four young adolescents. She was usually the only female on duty on her shift. The boys would have erections, either in the bathroom or the bedroom, subtly ensuring that Tina was near at hand while they pranced around naked or without pyjama trousers. One evening the oldest boy started to masturbate in her presence. Tina needed to share her reaction to this demonstration of adolescent sexuality but staff meetings at the assessment centre were devoted to administrative matters and supervision was infrequent and superficial. Tina knew from her observations that reporting the boys to senior staff would lead to swift and severe punishment, probably corporal, with no consideration given to a discussion and understanding of the underlying reasons for the boys' behaviour. She could not identify any staff member having the interest or ability to talk about masturbation with the boys. Tina could only contain her feelings and discuss them in the safety of the college setting.

Liz, also a CQSW student, was being shown around a community home by a 15-year-old boy Mark, on a pre-placement visit. They were walking along an upstairs corridor when Mark asked Liz to 'wait a moment' as he hurried into one of the bedrooms. Within seconds he called her into the bedroom where, on entering, she found him standing naked. Calmly she ignored his tentative advances and suggested that, when he had dressed, they would resume the tour. This he did and they walked around the rest of the school as if nothing had happened. Liz added an amusing touch. As she left Mark to return to the principal's office, she remarked, 'Thank you, Mark. That was an interesting visit. I think that you have shown me everything.' The boy grinned.

This was only an observation placement, Liz felt unsure of staff reaction, did not want the boy to be punished and only shared the incident with the consultant to the school a few days before she left. Mark maintained a friendly relationship with Liz during the period of her short stay but she felt unable to broach the subject with him. I am sure that, having talked about Mark's action with the consultant, this would have been her next step had she been remaining longer in the school.

Sue was 'needled' by Eric, a physically well-developed boy of 15 years, during the whole of the first month of her new job in a boys' hostel. He often set others against her. At the time Sue did not know that she was the first female member of staff, other than the warden's wife, ever to be employed there. One evening Eric wandered into the office where Sue was alone and engaged her in conversation for a few minutes. Suddenly he said, 'You want me to screw you, don't you? If you let me, I'll see that you get a quiet life.' Sue acknowledged the proposal and the comment – the 'want' and the 'let' conveyed a double message – and, as far as an excited Eric would allow, talked the matter through with him. Later, in the silence of her room, she began to shake and cried anxiously.

In a calmer frame of mind the next day Sue was able to use her period of supervision to talk about the conversation with Eric, and with her supervisor rehearsed the points that had to be raised first in staff discussion and then in the community meeting. In the latter, there was no direct reference to the previous evening although most of the boys had some ideas about what had taken place. Other matters allowed questions of aggression, bullying and intimidation to be aired and Eric responded to the signals emitted by staff and boys.

After a further month in the hostel Sue was able to spend time with Eric on his own in what amounted to sexual counselling, enabling him without embarrassment to share his ignorance of basic sexual facts, eventually helping him to find a girlfriend and to engage in a sexual relationship without threats and aggression.

Male members of staff are also quickly caught up in intimate exchanges. *Phil* was 21 years of age when he went into a residential special school for younger boys as a member of the care staff. He worked well, was efficient and popular. Being touched affectionately by 9- and 10-year-olds was a new experience for him but Phil become rather worried when three of the boys sought him out on their own or in pairs and wanted to kiss him, and did so frequently. He was both excited and distressed by the feelings that welled up inside him but there was nobody with whom these could be shared. His responsive close physical contact with the boys, for example, in the bath – 'interfering' in legal terms? – never became known and subsequently Phil moved on for training before taking up an appointment in fieldwork. Only later did he realise how his relationships with the boys would have been viewed had they ever come to light. Retrospectively, he saw himself at the age of 21 as in full adolescence, naïve, and effectively seduced by the physical exchanges initiated by the boys.

These accounts demonstrate a range of responses to the sexuality of young people in residential care. Joy, Liz and Sue were strengthened in their understanding; Tina left her placement disconcerted and dissatisfied; and Phil was lucky. Individually, Alan and Eric received help in growing up; Mark encountered someone able to set limits without punishing him; and the other boys were left with adults who, through no fault of their own, failed to draw boundaries or to use the experiences of daily living as points for discussion. The above illustrations show the value of individual and group supervision as vehicles for the understanding and management of young people's sexuality but, regrettably, also offer examples of children's centres where a denial of sexuality is still the first refuge, punishment the second and a forum for the regular examination of resident–staff exchanges, including those of a sexual nature, is not available.

Adolescent sexual development
I see the sexual education and almost inevitable experimentation of adolescents in care as a time for learning how to handle feelings,

how to make appropriate responses and how to prepare for a world of sexuality which they will otherwise meet abruptly, secretively and without preparation and protection. Too many establishments regard themselves as the last bastions of moral concern where adolescent sexuality is suppressed in a way no longer prevalent in the world outside. This is especially damaging among young people who have heightened awareness, are often touch-hungry, but who lack accurate information and the ability to control feelings.

This expression of sexuality is all the more likely with young people in residential care in the face of the distress and uncertainty brought about by the abnormality of their environment. The intimacy of group living engenders many of the conditions from which the problems emerge. Unfortunately, too few homes and residential schools are prepared – in either sense – to discuss healthily the sex-related difficulties. Subsequent condemnation and overloading with guilt only serve as a reflection of staff fears and inadequacies.

One of my most powerful recollections as a junior member of staff was witnessing the semi-public haranguing at breakfast time as 'dirty little beasts' of two 13-year-old boys found together in bed in an assessment centre. The head of home's voice was filled with venom, and with fear. The boys had removed their pyjama trousers and were engaged in mutual masturbation. Such an incident, as residential staff know, is a not uncommon occurrence. I appreciate the problems some staff have in responding other than with anger. The young people are presenting themselves in a different light – as pulsating, sexual beings exploring their capacities for sensual pleasure. Apart from all that has been said previously in this chapter about touch and sexuality, basic texts on human growth and behaviour regard such actions as a natural part of development. What was achieved – what is achieved? – by making the boys experience guilt and temporary if not lasting ostracism?

We do need to defend young people against those whose own anxieties, irregularly constructed moral codes or panic at the strength of their own feelings bring about a climate of suspicion and guilt. This does nothing to help adolescents on their path towards relationship-building and sexual maturation, on their road to perceiving and experiencing their sexuality as one of the most positive and fulfilling forces in their lives. We somehow have soft pink notions of 'relationships' and 'love' and 'affection' but shudder at and reject sex-linked experimentation and expression, thus seeking to make of people inhuman beings.

The primary task of the social worker confronted with the complexities of a young person's sexuality – whether this manifests itself as a developmental problem or as an issue causing moral conflict or practical difficulties to adults – is to ensure that he or she moves into adulthood potentially capable of sexual maturity and the full realisation of his or her sexual self. Most young people I have known – in care and out of care, on supervision orders or on care orders – have inbuilt discriminatory powers about sex and their sexual partners. The 'power' of the institution or adult authority that is not respected will rarely make an adolescent boy or an adolescent girl change an established pattern of sexual behaviour, and the pattern is often well established by the time that it is of sufficient concern to become the responsibility of a social worker to intervene. Heavy-handedness – and I use this word advisedly – may drive it underground, may confirm in a young person's mind the 'nasty' messages about sex that have for too long been received and may add more weight to the odds against successful functioning later in life. What is appreciated is information, and the support and counselling of a trusted, knowledgeable and sexually aware social worker, heterosexual or homosexual, male or female, who, above all, feels comfortable with the sexual side of his or her own being.

3 Adult Sexuality

While further comment will be made in Chapter 7 about the concept of 'maturity', an ideal mature sexual relationship between two adults may be perceived as one in which both find continuing satisfaction and fulfilment, are perfectly at ease with each other's bodies, constantly seek new and tiny demonstrations of care and concern, feel able to initiate activity, respond naturally and willingly and, during intercourse, endeavour to achieve a balance between the stimulation of their partner to a peak of sexual feeling and the 'selfish' enjoyment of the pleasure which, in turn, is offered. It is a relationship free from blackmail or bargaining, stemming from an equal power base. There are no rights or wrongs, do's or dont's, merely definition and redefinition of boundaries in the light of physical, emotional, and sometimes spiritual needs.

The extent to which this ideal is starry-eyed and more suitable for inclusion in the pages of a sex manual – and this has been suggested to me – is for each individual to decide. For many people the reality of the quality of their sexual relationships is far from the above description. Too often heterosexual intercourse occurs because the female 'gives in'; or because the male needs to find a channel for the expression of his authority and aggression; or he becomes overwhelmed by the intensity of his penial urges; or the act becomes a ritual to keep a relationship going; or two people just do not comprehend the significance and destructive potential of sexual exchanges.

Nevertheless, understanding can grow as each partner seeks with sensitivity to bring about the fulfilment of the other. Certainly, if maturity refers to real rather than ideal behaviour – a point acknowledged in Chapter 7 – people must be displaying degrees of maturity in their very struggle with the earthy and human deficiencies mentioned in the previous paragraph.

The extent to which a satisfying sexual relationship flows naturally from the love of one human being for another, or grows into love through a physical exchange, is arguable. While casual sexual relationships do provide temporary solace and comfort for some people – and, I would suggest, are increasingly part of the present approach to the management of personal relationships – ultimately a physical exchange is rarely on its own sufficient to sustain a relationship, although its initial excitement and stimulation may provide the basis and momentum for facets of personality, possible compatibility as companions, and mutual concerns and interests to be explored.

Sex is about giving and receiving, and within a sexual relationship two people may mirror much of their everyday lives. The satisfactions and dissatisfactions of their existence as a couple, and sometimes of their relationships with others in the family, their workplaces or the local community may be reflected in their most intimate sexual acts. Physical health affects a sexual relationship as does any temporary or semi-permanent emotional upset in one or both partners. Suspicion, too, may prevent a man or woman from finding relaxation and contentment in a sexual relationship, and the knowledge that a person is currently having – or has recently had – sex with another person may limit satisfaction in intercourse. The surroundings are important. Warmth, privacy and the security of knowing that love play and intercourse are unlikely to be interrupted all contribute to the increased possibility of an ease of physical and sexual exchange.

Physical and emotional problems

Poor standards of personal hygiene in the male or female – an unwashed or infected vagina, or excessive smegma under the foreskin of an uncircumcised penis – may make intercourse an unattractive proposition, while not necessarily lessening the desire for release but increasing the frustration. The age of the couple, and the difference in their ages, may over time change their sexual appetite and their sexual behaviour. Frequent penetration may give way to more stroking and caressing. For some masturbation may be an acceptable alternative or addition to intercourse. The nature of sexuality, the way that a person's ability to express it is so linked with the past, the extent to which the quality of the experience in a strong relationship often only grows with time and the manner in which comparatively tiny disturbances can upset the balance of a sexual relationship make sexual activity an area of study and understanding to which social workers should be fully attuned. They cannot work with adults, or indeed with any clients, without a knowledge of sexual games, sexual politics, sexual drives, sexual dysfunction and sexual satisfactions.

Within the context of their work with adults social workers may find themselves concerned with any aspect of their clients' sexuality – physical, emotional or moral. They may be called upon to address in some detail the physical and emotional problems surrounding a sexual relationship. They may need to work across the boundaries of both heterosexual and homosexual relationships; with a range of handicapped people; with the most intimate physical problems of both males and females experiencing unsatisfactory sexual intercourse; and with residents in homes too frequently denied the opportunity for sexual expression merely because of the accommodation provided or the attitudes of some residential staff who control major parts of their lives. Sometimes clients and residents will readily bring to a discussion their sex-related problems, while others will require considerable help and opportunities to talk without feeling 'bad', guilty or that it is wrong to express their anger, anxiety, frustration or fears about sexual relationships.

Some problems are primarily of a medical nature and may be best tackled exclusively by a general practitioner, or sometimes in partnership with a social worker. Vaginal infections, for example, do cause considerable irritation, may lessen the drive for intercourse and, for a while, may even make it inadvisable. Social workers attached to a health centre are especially well placed to become involved in sexual counselling and in the emotionally-related problems arising from infected sexual organs, sexual dysfunction, impotence, the inability of a woman to conceive or the practical difficulties associated with the use of a particular method of contraception. For instance, a man may lose his erection in pausing to put on a sheath, and thus become anxious about his masculinity; or, again, either a man or a woman may be uncertain about how to behave sexually during menstruation. Most sexually active couples work out and work at problems intuitively, by reference to books – or never even acknowledge minor difficulties as problems, just working naturally towards a resolution. For many others, however, problems are not immediately or gently resolved, do produce considerable tension and anguish, and require sympathetic analysis, advice, counselling and practical help. For the majority of the population sex is a very private affair – sometimes harmonious, sometimes disastrous. Other people – by choice, by opportunity or as a sequel to contact with a social worker – have a third person drawn in to help unravel their sexual complexities.

Social work intervention
Within a casework relationship questions may arise about conception, contraception and infertility. A woman may blame her husband for his seeming inability to make her pregnant; or she may fear being made pregnant; or he may place all responsibility for

contraception on his wife; or both may be tortured by their frequent desires for sexual intercourse but be unwilling to go against their religious beliefs which forbid the use of contraceptives. There may be residual blame for an earlier unwanted pregnancy, guilt about an abortion hurriedly arranged at a time of crisis or fears about giving birth to a handicapped child because of genetic uncertainties on either side of the family. Emotional blockages may be found in relation to past events. A young woman at the start of her first adult sexual relationship may relive with terror an incestuous exchange which took place five years previously; a man buggered in adolescence may secretly desire anal intercourse with his wife, but fear rejection if he attempts to penetrate her in this way. Sometimes either males or females may struggle with questions of sexual orientation, taking years to confirm themselves as heterosexual or to acknowledge their homosexuality and their preference and need for a partner of the same sex, even though they may have fathered or mothered a child meanwhile.

There may be anxieties between a couple as the boundaries of sexual exchanges are explored. An experienced male partner may accept and expect oral exchanges, to be masturbated by his partner, to watch his partner masturbate or to help her come to a climax manually; he may wish to experiment with a variety of positions; or, as suggested, to have anal intercourse. The speed, insistence and insensitivity of a man's demands may cause a wife to withdraw, to dread the marriage bed and sometimes feel unable to bear her husband touching her.

A woman may find difficulty in responding sexually to her husband if his fantasies fill her with nausea and disgust. Diana recalled the events leading to her gradual alienation from her husband:

At first the main problem was his sexual deviations. He wanted me to do weird things like sleeping with other men. He wanted me especially to have oral sex with them so that he could watch. He once brought a man home so that he could look at me while I sucked his penis. I was so sickened that after a few minutes I ran down the road to a neighbour's house . . . He kept a cupboard in our bedroom locked. One day I broke it open. There were several pairs of knickers which he said he had taken off washing lines in the neighbourhood and piles of books about sex, mostly what you would call 'hard porn' with pictures of people masturbating or having intercourse, and men having sex with children. At night in bed all these pictures came into my mind . . .

Diana eventually ran away from her husband. Although not brutal, his sexual demands became more and more regarded by his wife as rape. Earlier mutual desire became dulled by the excesses of the male, and Diana no longer accepted the fantasy world of her husband. She became unable to receive him, her vagina felt tight and dry, and she opened her legs as an act of compassion or just to prevent a quarrel. Intercourse was painful, she felt sore afterwards and cried with loathing and dismay as he ejaculated and withdrew. Sexually she could neither give nor receive.

Women, of course, may use their power to tease a man, to arouse him sexually and then refuse to allow penetration, causing emotional and physical stress leading to intolerable frustration. A man may also be made to feel sexually inferior – because he fails to maintain an erection, ejaculates prematurely or is said by his wife not to give her any satisfaction. A woman may worry about her inability to have an orgasm; or be concerned that while masturbating alone she reaches a climax without difficulty, but in the presence of her husband takes much longer. Some women worry about what they perceive as their own sexual deviations. Doreen hesitated for some time before telling her husband that, during her separations from him – he was often away at work overnight – she used a candle to provide stimulation and satisfaction as she masturbated.

In working with couples whose problems are sexual in origin the first task is to get them to talk freely – about their satisfactions, about the fears, about their hopes, about their difficulties and about their seeming incompatibility. They may initially need to talk without the other partner present. Enabling people to express themselves in an uninhibited way about very personal matters may take time. Every other aspect of their lives may be presented as the basis for their disagreements. Many of these, for example financial, concerning leisure activities or drinking habits, may really be the sources of contention, while other disagreements will undoubtedly stem from unresolved sexual dilemmas or misunderstandings.

Writing about anxiety in everyday life, Eric Trimmer, a general practitioner, reflects upon the fear of reality; in one case history he illustrates several of the points that have been raised earlier and identifies a particular way in which one wife endeavoured to withdraw from the intimacy of marriage:

A woman of thirty, who was married and had two children, sought advice because of her self-confessed frigidity. She maintained that although she loved her husband, sexual intercourse never interested her. Her sexual coldness had driven her husband to various irregular sex liaisons. Rather than provoke endless argument she had, for many years, condoned his behaviour. Recently however she was becoming worried about her spouse's heavy drinking. Apparently the friend he associated with in his sexual pursuits had a bad influence on him in other ways as well, and was getting him into debt. At a confrontation the husband agreed to give up his extra-marital sexual activities if she would give the marriage a fresh start. Although she very much wanted to do this, her inherent frigidity put her in a terrible position.

The past history of this woman, as it emerged, was extremely interesting. Brought up by rich and rather authoritarian parents, she had been caught when quite young playing at some quite innocent sex game with a small boy cousin. The housekeeper who discovered this childhood episode of simple exploratory sex reported the whole thing to her father, who had reacted violently and quite unreasonably. For years afterwards she had felt herself 'watched over' very carefully by her parents, and was not allowed to go out with friends of the opposite sex at all until she had left school.

She expressed the thought that her parents obviously believed she was a 'sex maniac' of some sort, for they lost no opportunity of discussing, in her presence, any incident that was locally known or was to be found in the newspapers, which demonstrated the 'terrors of sex', and the unworthiness of all sexual experience.

During all this time she admitted to being fascinated with everything that had sexual overtones. She borrowed such erotic literature from school friends as was obtainable, and derived intense satisfaction from the casual sexual interest shown to her by boy friends. All this time, however, she was strongly aware that sex was an absolutely taboo, forbidden subject, at any rate before marriage.

When she met her husband, who was considered very suitable by her parents, the courtship was a whirlwind one and they were married without there being anything very much in the way of sexual knowledge between them. Then, to use her own words, 'sex suddenly died' for her. When her husband made love to her she suffered extreme palpitation and 'thought she would expire'. She never reached orgasm and found the whole experience revolting and curiously frustrating. When asked what palpitation meant, she defined it as 'the sort of heart action that occurs shortly before death'. (She had, in fact, had an aunt who suffered from cardiac failure when she was a child, and this woman often took her hand and placed it on her chest to 'feel how bad' her heart was.)

This case proved very difficult to treat and reference to psychiatric colleagues was singularly unhelpful. Very slowly, however, she improved, after accepting that her symptoms were those of anxiety, produced in her mind by a conditioning process during her childhood and adolescence.

It was explained that a dominating belief had been implanted in her mind during her young days that could be summed up by the phrase, 'sex is forbidden'. As she grew up, however, she was naturally drawn by curiosity to this forbidden subject. Eventually she made a bargain with herself. Her natural sexual drives, which were strong, were in fact forbidden drives and the fascination of them, as a young, developing woman, sprang from their forbidden quality. On marriage she discovered that sex was, patently, not forbidden. The reality of a normal sexual relationship became very unattractive to her, and this made her very anxious.

Her anxiety symptoms were really produced by the unnerving position in which she eventually found herself – that was, married to a man for whom she had no sexual feeling or inclination. Subconsciously, then, she protected herself by a screen of real illness. She knew that someone with a bad heart suffered from palpitations. Naturally therefore, she told herself the palpitations she felt when her husband made love to her might kill her, and therefore coitus could be abandoned legitimately.

By this neurotic logic she convinced herself that she could not be expected to take her rightful place in her marriage. In a nutshell, fear of her real situation, that is, she was a married woman who should reasonably be expected to make love to her husband, made her so anxious that it drove her to develop psychosomatic symptoms, in this case palpitation, that could excuse her from playing her proper role in life.[1]

Relationships within marriage

Jack Dominian suggests that, in marriage, each act of sexual intercourse is preceded by the accumulated inter-personal contact of weeks, months and years. A wife's feelings, he says, may be expressed by refusal, indifference or failure to appreciate her husband's effort. He describes how, in the case of one couple who sought help, the wife never refused her husband intercourse but she had driven him to distraction by looking at the ceiling and never at him when they were having sex. It later emerged that during intercourse she looked for and counted cobwebs on the walls and ceiling. Dominian goes on to summarise in a piece of imaginary writing what he perceives as the complaints of many husbands all over the world:[2]

To my ever-loving wife,
During the past year I have attempted to seduce you 365 times. I succeeded 36 times. This averages once every ten days, and the following is a list of excuses made on the unsuccessful occasions:

We will wake the children	7	The baby is crying	18
It's too hot	15	Watched late show	7
It's too cold	3	Watched early show	5
Too tired	19	Mudpack on	12
It's too late	16	Grease on face	6
It's too early	9	Reading Sunday paper	10
Pretending to sleep	33	You are too drunk	9
Windows are open,		We have company in the	
neighbours will hear	3	next room	7
Your back ached	16	Your parents were staying	
Toothache	2	with us	5
Headache	26	My parents were staying	
Giggling fit	2	with us	5
I've had too much	4	Is that all you ever think	
Not in the mood	21	about	105

Do you think you could improve our record this coming year?
Your ever-loving husband,

Social workers may need to help couples in some detail with their sexual problems, pinpointing the difficulties they experience, offering practical suggestions for improving their sex life and 'giving permission' for new approaches to intercourse. There are now numerous manuals available to which reference can be made and it may be useful for a couple to share the contents of these, the illustrations themselves providing a stimulus for erotic love-making. As Dominian says, 'negative feelings are not the sole prerogative of the wife' and I would very much like to see a complementary list compiled by a woman. Where would the male be found wanting?

Tension within one partner is often a barrier to good sex. A relaxed approach, therefore, may be an essential preliminary for some couples: they may need to move towards full intercourse at a much slower pace; gentle massage of each other's body, avoiding the genital areas for as long as possible may help arousal; sharing fantasies may be mutually exciting; varying the amount of light in the room may bring about a change of mood; and watching each other masturbate may be satisfying and stimulating. In general, men quite unashamedly enjoy their sex, once they have got over any early fear about actually being able to perform. They expect to enjoy sex. They may be able to obtain added pleasure from thinking more about the pleasure of their partner. Women may sometimes need encouragement to acknowledge their right to enjoy themselves and to give full expression to their sexuality. They may need to think more about creating opportunities to masturbate while on their own, giving free rein to their fantasies, exploring their bodies and gaining skills in bringing themselves to a climax, allowing themselves the 'selfish' enjoyment to which I referred earlier. For couples seriously concerned to improve the quality of their sex life, or to rekindle it, a determination to provide maximum erotic stimulation for the partner and to indicate new ways of sharing mind and body is often the way to more mutually exciting sexual intercourse.

In all sexual counselling the social worker must be aware of difficulties arising from the cultural origin of the couple, or of one partner. In some minority groups the sexual liberation of the woman advocated above would not be recognised. In addition to Protestants, Roman Catholics and Jews, social workers have increasingly to think about sex and birth control in relation to other religious groups, for example Buddhists, Hindus, followers of Islam and the Eastern Orthodox Church, all of which have fundamentally different values and attitudes.[3]

Sometimes, however, a woman's notions of romantic love will have died, nothing stirs in her genital area in response to her husband's overtures, she feels trapped economically and by the children for whom she feels love and responsibility, while her husband's needs for sexual relief build up inside him night after night. The woman may be willing to offer comfort and companionship, but remain unable to be a participant in the erotic exchanges to which her husband aspires. Both will have their frustrations. Both will have their fantasies. He may become increasingly violent, find a girlfriend outside the marriage or seek the services of a prostitute. She, in turn, may find a lover and a new sexual awakening. There is a feeling of inevitability about later separation when earlier mutual attraction dies within one partner and there is no joint will to try again. At best, and sometimes only for the sake of the children, the couple will continue to live under the same roof. Often a double bed is replaced by twin beds, and sometimes ultimately by separate rooms. The social work task will sometimes be to help two people to separate – with the minimum amount of pain.

At times of separation, when sexual incompatibility is apparent, a client may wish to recall the past, confirming himself or herself as a sexual being, obtaining acknowledgement of having sexually satisfied a partner in the past and wanting hope and reassurance that the delights of sexual intercourse will be there to experience again in the future. As a man it is difficult, perhaps impossible, to comprehend female sexuality to the full, yet women sometimes prefer talking to a man about former partners. Angela never regarded herself as a lesbian, but needed to share any residual doubts before moving on to enjoy a new and, as it turned out, long-lasting relationship. Starting at a college of education at 19 years of age was for Angela much lonelier than she had anticipated. She was 150 miles from home, had had a strict upbringing and felt acutely the absence of the limited physical contact she had enjoyed with boy-friends from the evangelical church community in her home town. Although still sexually inexperienced she had drawn comfort and warmth from the fondling that had taken place, and increasingly felt the need to express herself through her body. A young female tutor at the college was soon attracted to her, and they took every opportunity to share a bed:

> It felt very little different from sleeping with a man. I needed comforting and stroking. The warmth was the same. The pleasure from caressing each other's vagina was intense. I was much less experienced than Monique. I never had an orgasm with her although we both masturbated each other. Only later did I realise that she must have had frequent orgasms as we lay there naked, each desperate for the other, but perhaps for different reasons.

Five years later, and married with a young daughter, Angela thought about this earlier relationship – at a period in her life when sexual intercourse with her husband had deteriorated to the point of being 'a painful ritual to be finished as quickly as possible'. For Angela, as with Diana, this was the nearest thing to rape that she had experienced.

Sexual violence
Again, as a man, I feel unqualified to write at length about rape. Any physical assault on another human being can leave permanent scars of mind and body. When such an assault violently – and without concern – penetrates the parts of the body reserved for what should be the most intimate and pleasurable contact of a person's existence, then such violation should not go unchecked and un-punished. Many incidents of sexual assault are not reported, leaving unresolved anger and fears. Present approaches to questioning; to medical examinations; and to court appearances often only add to stress, and do little to encourage victims to name their assailants. Gradually, however, rape crisis centres – staffed by both volunteers and professional workers – are being set up, providing legal

support, medical advice and counselling. Details of the London Rape Crisis Centre are given towards the end of this book.

Ideally every social services department should have a rape crisis centre, offering without militancy and without the subtle messages tending to bring about the further alienation of women from men, the most skilled social work practice. Crisis intervention is one of the most important areas of social work. In cases of rape it calls for even higher levels of sensitivity and concern. What does come within my experience is the number of women, like Diana and Angela, trapped by marriage, who are 'legally raped' by their husbands night after night, sometimes until they can bear the pain and humiliation no longer. There is a move afoot to make it possible for a case of rape to be brought within the marital relationship. A change in the law cannot come soon enough. Men may then have to think much more about 'giving' rather than 'receiving' pleasure within a sexual relationship. Paradoxically, only then may some learn what sex is all about.

Sex and elderly people
For the most part we choose to ignore the sexual interests and sexual needs of elderly people. Just as it is difficult for some adults and young people to imagine their parents enjoying sex, so the denial of the possibility of a sex life is transferred to elderly clients. This, of course, is often very far from the truth. While some elderly people do experience a decline in sexual activity with advancing years this is by no means universally so and McCary concludes that physiologically 'there is little reason – short of actual disease – for an older man or woman not to enjoy an active sex life, even if it must be a relatively modified one.'[4] He suggests that marital coitus among older men and their wives occurs considerably more frequently than is commonly realised and quotes a figure of 48 per cent for men between the ages of 75 and 92 who are capable of satisfactory sexual experience. McCary also points to the lack of evidence that ageing produces 'any decline in the sexual capacity of women until, possibly, quite late in life' (pp. 53–4).

In working with elderly clients in their own homes, perhaps following loss and separation or with the onset of physical disability, the social worker should more frequently think about their frustration or depression in terms of their sexual feelings. Some workers may be reluctant to broach this as a cause of personal difficulty or unhappiness, but the fantasy world of an elderly man or woman may still be as rich and compelling as that of a younger person:

. . . older people *do* have sexual yearnings, and these desires are perfectly normal. Is it any wonder, though, that the older person is frequently bewildered by his sexual drive and is ashamed of it? The Victorian ethic pervading American sexual mores [and English culture!] says that he should live in a sexless vacuum. His children very likely say, voicelessly, 'Sex is for the young. Act your age.' And it is entirely possible that the physician compounds his elderly patient's confusion and bewilderment by answering any questions having to do with sex by saying, 'Well, what do you expect at your age?' Unless a physician is convinced of the psychological importance of sexual expression in the later years of life, he can do irreparable damage to his geriatric patient's sexuality, to say nothing of his general mental and physical health . . . Since there is so much to be gained from continued sexual activity and since intercourse is certainly physically possible in the later years of life, why, then, do so many older people shrink from it? For many of them, the popular attitude that the older person is sexless becomes a self-fulfilling prophecy.

(McCary, pp. 56–7)

Elderly people may manage and enjoy a whole range of sexual activities until quite late in life, sharing their bodies in any way they wish behind the closed doors of their own homes. It is not, however, until an elderly person or an elderly couple are admitted to a residential home that sexual 'problems' may sometimes become apparent, and these difficulties may be solely the result of living in the new environment. They may, in effect, be the problems of the care givers and the other residents, and not of the individuals concerned.

Some elderly people admitted to residential homes may not perceive any limitations resulting from their new environment. They may, in fact, see the home as offering new opportunities. A man, for example, apart from occasionally 'touching up' one of the other residents, may find a partner for regular sex. This needs a careful response – and sometimes an element of control – from members of staff. Avoidance of coarse humour is important. The deputy head of a residential unit showing me around could only make a jocular, and rather ribald remark to an elderly but sprightly male as he hurried out of a woman resident's room tucking in his shirt and pulling up the zip of his trousers.

More seriously, the following were described to me towards the end of last year by the heads and deputies of two residential homes as very pressing problems in their establishments. I am outlining the three cases in the present tense, as they were put to me, and invite readers to think about their own responses and possible solutions. The actual outcomes will be given subsequently.

Case 1 Ann, 80 years of age, has been living in a home for just over six months. She is active, has a degree in psychology and is articulate. On several occasions other female residents have complained about her behaviour, alleging that she pinches their bottoms, puts her hand on their knees, tries to hold their hands or gives them a tender embrace, especially when she finds a resident on her own. She has several times been openly referred to as a lesbian, and is gradually being rejected by other residents. On many occasions the staff have found Ann sobbing in her room. They, too, have found it more and more difficult to give her a hug or to kiss her good night in the same way that they approach other residents.

Case 2 Sam and Sarah are 86 and 85 years respectively, the two surviving members of a family in which there were 10 children. They lived together for more than 60 years before admission to a residential home in 1982 where it soon became apparent that they were continuing a long-standing incestuous relationship. They enjoy bathing each other, like looking at each other's naked body and spend some time each day lying together almost naked on the single bed in Sam's room. On two occasions there have been reports that they were fondling each other's genitals.

Case 3 Mr Jones – he is always called Mr Jones – came into a residential home following the demolition of his home after an articulated lorry had crashed through the lounge wall of his small rented property. He is 70 years of age, shy and not very communicative. Several days each week he receives a visit from a friend, a man of about 50 years. Mr Jones has, however, quietly and quite proudly told a number of people that for as long as he can remember the man who visits him has been his lover. The couple usually spend two or three hours together in Mr Jones's room when his friend visits him and he leaves a few minutes before the bell rings for tea.

Staff in residential homes for the elderly are more and more having to think about questions of sexuality, and some need a great deal of help in doing so. What happened to Ann, Sam and Sarah, and Mr Jones? Mr Jones had to be transferred within a few weeks to another home. He was driven out by the other residents who made constant bitter complaints that he was 'dirty' and that 'It shouldn't be allowed.' Mr Jones was eventually found a place in another home at his own request. The staff appeared to have no strong feelings about whether he stayed or went, but in the end Mr Jones would not leave his room, so great was the hostility of the other residents. Ann, on the other other, remained in the same home, was very accessible to counselling and wanted to talk at length about her past. She was still grieving the loss three years earlier of the friend she had lived with. They had enjoyed a lesbian relationship, and Ann could not cope with the absence from her life of frequent physical contact with another human being. Relationships for Ann within the home did remain tense until she found a constant companion who also needed greater intimacy in her life, and this helped both their relationships with the wider group. One member of the care staff was especially helpful to Ann. In addition to enabling her to talk freely about the enormous physical and emotional pleasures experienced earlier in her life, she encouraged her to start writing an autobiography, giving shape and purpose to a lifetime of passion and fulfilment. Life for Sam and Sarah changed very little. They were in time given slightly more suitable accommodation in a small annex to the main building. Ostensibly they had their individual rooms, although one contained a three-quarter sized bed, and some nights they spent together. The physical side of their relationship did not seem to worry other residents, and they may even not have known about it. Sam and Sarah were popular in the home and their brotherly and sisterly concern was seen as quite touching.

Even with seemingly straightforward heterosexual relationships between non-related adults the constraints of group living are often apparent. Hilary and Harry have lived in the psychogeriatric ward of a large hospital for a number of years. Hilary is blind. Although not married the couple believe themselves to be man and wife, are kind to each other and Harry is always on hand to help Hilary, for example at mealtimes. But there are rules by which the relationship is controlled: Harry is never allowed to tuck Hilary up in bed; and he is forbidden to accompany her to the toilet – which he does whenever he gets the chance. He reassures the staff. 'It's all right,' he says, 'When she takes her knickers down I look the other way.'

Relationships between elderly people are, however, much more complicated than this. In a recent placement study the dilemmas facing residential social workers caring for elderly people were well illustrated by one student, Elizabeth Gerard of Liverpool, who wrote as follows:

Bert was in his early eighties and had lived in residential care for four or five years. He was a tall, smart-looking man who had nursed his wife for a number of years prior to her death and was admitted to residential care because he no longer wished to live alone, though he was physically and mentally capable of living in the community with minimum support had he wished. Nancy was in her early sixties and was initially admitted to a home for elderly mentally infirm people, suffering from pre-senile dementia. She was later transferred to the old people's home where I was doing my placement though she was still in a confused state. However, by the time that I was introduced to Nancy she had improved considerably but nevertheless required a great deal of supervision. Nancy tended to have a blank expression on her face for the majority of the time but did have her lucid moments.

Bert started to take an interest in Nancy just a few weeks before my arrival at the home. He was very caring, for example, leading her to the dining room and assisting in cutting her food. This was helpful to both Nancy and the staff as Bert was able to give her individual attention. At this stage I thought that the relationship appeared positive and Bert had found an important role for himself as carer.

About five weeks later a member of staff reported to the head of the home that she had observed Bert and Nancy in a state of heavy petting in Nancy's bedroom, Bert's usual routine being to take tea around to some of the residents and to dress Nancy. A discussion then took place among the senior staff at which I was present and it was apparent that we had conflicting views on the issue. There were certain points to consider before any intervention took place:

1. Nancy and Bert appeared to be enjoying the relationship. It was giving Nancy individual attention which she could not obtain otherwise and was possibly meeting her sexual needs as it was thought that she had probably been used to regular sex before she became ill. It also met Bert's sexual needs and fulfilled his role as carer.

2. If Bert was requested not to have a sexual relationship with Nancy would he then withdraw altogether from the relationship which, in turn, may have had a negative effect on Nancy?

3. Nancy was unable to make a decision for herself and was therefore at risk of being taken advantage of sexually.

4. Nancy was admitted to a residential home in order to be cared for. Should the home subsequently protect her against such behaviour?

It was decided that the relationship between Bert and Nancy would be watched carefully, and staff would be told to dress and undress Nancy in order not to put Bert in the unfair position of tempting him. Staff would make discreet checks in the early morning in order to discourage Bert from going into Nancy's room.

A week or so later Nancy started to deteriorate and become distressed at night, hallucinating and appearing to be frightened. Medication was prescribed for night time only but she continued to deteriorate to the point where she was smearing faeces all over her bedroom. Her facial expression became permanently blank. Following assessment at a nearby psychogeriatric unit she was readmitted to a home for elderly mentally infirm residents.

The four points raised within the staff group do lead us to think about the rights of two adults to enjoy a sexual relationship if they so wish; about the possible effects of intervention; and about the mental capacity of a particular individual to make her own decisions. There is no complete answer. We have no right to stop the relationship merely because the staff members find it difficult to tolerate. Bert and Nancy were adults, albeit elderly residents. On the other hand, Nancy could be a relative of mine or yours, reader. A desire to 'protect' her from such activity would then, I guess, be uppermost in many people's minds.

In this chapter we have considered particularly the sexual difficulties of adults, noting ways in which problems manifest themselves and the fact that they may continue throughout life's span. They are often equally apparent, if we care to look, in elderly people. In many instances an adult is as fragile and vulnerable – although in a different manner – as an adolescent on the edge of sexual experience. In the face of blows to their sexual relationship, of hostility to their sexual orientation, or of a newly-experienced violent sexual exchange, adults may test the limits of their emotional resilience. Under such circumstances, the maturity of the social worker – able to set aside tendencies to voyeurism, to avoid acting out his or her own sexual fantasies, and to keep some bounds in enjoying 'too much' the opportunity to delve into the sex life of another person – is also put to the test. Anybody may be found wanting on occasion, and social workers are sexual beings.

4 Special Needs and Special Groups

I turn now to the needs of special groups, particularly people living in some form of residential accommodation, and later to one group of staff. The first point to emphasise is that the sexual urges and aspirations of most handicapped people are no less powerful than those of others. Their need for satisfaction and their desire for sexual relief are often just as pressing. An article I once wrote on this theme was aptly entitled – by someone else – 'Sex behind bars' and the first quotation I used was taken from the brilliant and disturbing novel by Albert Camus, *L'Etranger*, intended, some say, as a statement about the absurdity of mortal life.

Awaiting trial on a murder charge in Algiers, Meursault, the hero (or anti-hero) reflects on the first months of his incarceration:

> . . . I was plagued by the desire for a woman – which was natural enough, considering my age. I never thought of Marie especially. I was obsessed by thoughts of this woman or that, of all the ones I'd had, all the circumstances under which I'd loved them; so much so that the cell grew crowded with their faces, ghosts of my old passions . . . I gradually became quite friendly with my old gaoler . . . It was he who brought up the subject of women. 'That's what the men here grumble about most,' he told me. I said that I felt like that myself. 'There's something unfair about it,' I added, 'like hitting a man when he's down.' 'But that's the whole point of it,' he said: 'that's why you fellows are kept in prison.' 'I don't follow.' 'Liberty,' he said, 'means that. You're being deprived of your liberty.' It has never struck me before in that light but I saw his point. 'That's true,' I said. 'Otherwise it wouldn't be punishment.' The gaoler nodded. 'Yes, you're different, you can use your brains. The others can't. Still, these fellows find a way out; they do it themselves.' With which remark the gaoler left my cell. Next day I did like the others.[1]

In matters of sex in prison, society remains uncompromisingly harsh. Campaigns for conjugal visits meet with no success and it may well be beyond the turn of the century before we witness any universal change of attitudes.

Meanwhile, mentally and physically handicapped people (and I do have reservations about considering the two groups together) often fare as badly as Meursault. For those in residential care, the structures, routines and organisation of the establishments in which they live – not on criminal charges but supposedly as equal members of our society – are largely geared towards the imprisonment of sexuality within their bodies, where it remains locked in by prejudice. Families, too, frequently deny or repress the sexuality of their handicapped members.

The taboos surrounding sex and handicapped people are, for the most part, as strong as ever. Myth and fantasy linger; we make little effort to enter generously into the intimate world of the bizarre and the deformed. Many are no less tormented than Meursault. Ann Shearer points out that of all the problems handicapped people face in our society, sexual and emotional ones are the least discussed:

> We either deny that they have such 'normal' feelings at all, or make sure (in our financial, physical and social provision for them) that they will find it hard to express them. We deny them the fulfilment of marriage and children on the grounds that they couldn't cope; yet we would be properly horrified if anyone suggested that the children of broken homes, or people on low wages, should be barred from marriage, even though their difficulties in coping are far better documented than those we choose to call 'disabled' . . . The only difference between the handicapped population and the rest may be in the methods of fulfilment; yet we accept a variety of emotional and sexual expression in the rest of the population, we deny its properness here.[2]

But yet there is hope. The attitudes of some staff groups are changing and rising levels of understanding accompany falling levels of embarrassment. This in itself, however, may only achieve a marginal shift in practice. Without the unequivocal support of management outside the establishment in the acknowledgement of a sexual dimension to the lives of handicapped people, basic care staff rest on a knife edge, both in relation to innovation and to the dilemmas of their own consciences.

Meursault was denied the sexual expression which he longed for because of his conflict with the law, the confines of his prison cell, and the attitudes of his gaolers and their masters. Those in our midst who are mentally and physically handicapped have committed no crime, and ostensibly we seek to provide living conditions as far removed as possible from the prison model of the past.

Where does the conflict lie? Primarily, I suggest, it is within ourselves. Too often we collude with the assumptions of asexuality of handicapped people and link emotional difficulties and odd behaviour to problems of personality, or ascribe 'deviancy' to what elsewhere would pass unnoticed.

This is sad when one of the principal needs is to break into the voyeuristic displays of the popular press which feed an ignorant, and outwardly prudish, public. If we can turn the vigour with which the media hunt sexual scandals in residential settings into a campaign to establish the rights of handicapped residents, then management and elected representatives might become less sensitive to criticism when varied approaches to the provision of opportunities for individually satisfying lifestyles throw up politically delicate questions.

Sex and physically handicapped people

The sexual needs of physically handicapped people should, therefore, be an area of particular concern both to fieldworkers working with clients in their own homes and to residential social workers responsible for the more intimate aspects of their lives. Often the idea of copulation between those with severe, or even mild, handicap, or of assistance by a third party in the sexual act, is regarded with abhorrence or coarse humour. In an article on sex counselling for those with spinal injuries,[3] Isaacson and Delgado draw attention to evidence accumulated since 1950 which indicates that the loss of sexual function is far less prevalent than had been believed. The authors quote studies which demonstrate the injustice of imputing universal impotence to male patients and confirm that intercourse and conception are usually possible for disabled women. In condemning social work practice which fails to give sufficient acknowledgement to the fact that sexuality is a central characteristic of human affairs they suggest that:

> Owing to their physical limitations, persons with spinal cord injuries have been seen as passive, dependent individuals who could not perform sexually. Because of this feeling, health professionals have believed that repressive and suppressive psychological processes should be encouraged as a means of limiting patients' thoughts about an active sex life. This approach to the subject is understandable in light of the fact that, in the past, repression of sexuality was a part of the prevailing mores. It does not, however, serve the current generation, which has been raised with fewer inhibitions and less emphasis on repression of sexual thoughts and feelings. (p. 623)

The same thought is taken up by Miller and Gwynne in their study of residential establishments for physically handicapped people. They report commonly-held attitudes against the development of heterosexual pair relationships between residents; which rule out marriage between residents as a matter of policy; and which uphold active measures to segregate the men from the women. In this way an atmosphere is built up within an establishment wherein residents tend 'to take on the value system that suggests that marriage, or a mature heterosexual relationship without the legal tie, is the preserve of the able-bodied.'[4]

Such attitudes militate against the broad caring function which residential staff set out to provide, and deny to physically handicapped people basic choices in human functioning. Often the message is best conveyed through the words of an individual struggling to be like everybody else, and one of the most telling comments I know is offered in illustration by Wendy Greengross in her book *Entitled to Love*:

> For as long as I can remember I have been conscious of two me's – the outer casing which is visible to the world and the inner substance which is not. The outer casing is of course my body and is the façade by which in all but a few circumstances the world judges me. The inner part is my mind, my character, my conscience and my true being. Take away my twisted limbs, peel off my peculiar facial expressions and remove all traces of my athetoid condition and you will be left with a normal man.[5]

Isaacson and Delgado call for a comprehensive sex education and counselling programme for physically handicapped people given by those with a mature sexual adjustment themselves and able to deal frankly with the subject in a relaxed manner. The importance of including the partner is underlined together with the need to examine the place of physical satisfaction *vis-à-vis* that of emotional and psychological satisfaction. In practical terms, Isaacson and Delgado draw attention to two categories of physically handicapped people. The first includes those who no longer have the capacity or ability to manage intercourse and need help in working out alternative methods of satisfying partner and self. The second group consists of those for whom intercourse is possible but who need assistance with positioning and other adaptive measures.[6]

How far do these ideas fit in with current approaches in residential social work? The following illustrates how one member of staff made his own decisions about the needs of someone for whom he cared:

> John, 23 years of age, had worked for two years as a care assistant in a home for severely physically handicapped people, and had recently married. He enjoyed an easy relationship with Ted, an intelligent 17-year-old resident who at times became overwhelmingly frustrated and depressed because of the serious nature of his handicap and partial paralysis. In the course of the intimate care which John had to give Ted as

part of his duties, the latter prevailed upon John to masturbate him from time to time. The fact became known within the home.

The reactions of the head of home, the homes manager, the field social worker, other members of staff, social services committee members and other residents in the home produced forceful comments varying from uncompromising condemnation to sympathetic approval. Only the residents and a limited number of staff seemed able to appreciate the anxieties sustained by John and Ted both before and after the facts became known. Sincerely held opinions of the 'onlookers' had to be respected and evaluated, but whose lives were affected? What was 'deviant' in this instance? Certainly, if we believe in basic rights for human beings, there is no justification for withholding them in the residential setting. Indeed, to do so must be viewed as malpractice. This has implications for the training of staff, for the support of staff and for sex education programmes for physically handicapped children and young people. Do we pay lip service to sex education as a young person moves from childhood through adolescence and into adulthood, talking in biological and intellectual terms, then forever deny to him or her full physical sensations? Because nature has determined that we have to have physical care – and apparent custody – of physically handicapped people does this give us licence to control the sexual satisfactions which they may enjoy? Most 14- and 15-year-old boys find frequent sexual relief in masturbation. Not far from where I live is a young man, by now probably 16 years of age, and he has no arms. By any standards he is a handsome boy, well groomed and well dressed, cared for by loving parents and socially well able to manage his disability. I have often wondered, though, and particularly in drafting this chapter, about any sexual tensions he has experienced in growing up and the help he has received in relieving them.

Physical handicap and sex education
The sex education of all physically disabled children and young people presents problems. The sex education of blind children presents particular problems. Helping them to understand how their bodies work, and how the bodies of members of the opposite sex work requires patience, skill and confidence on the part of those responsible for their personal and educational development, whether parents or substitute care givers. Young people who are blind should be able to enjoy the excitement of their growing bodies

and the associated sexual awareness, whether of growing breasts or pubic hair, the shape of the vagina or an erect penis, but will lack an essential faculty – sight – which would enable them to match their bodies against those of members of the opposite sex. Touch, there-fore, becomes even more important because without it the young blind person has no way of making comparisons or understanding similarity or difference. Greengross reports that in Sweden blind children are given the opportunity to touch living naked bodies, both male and female, so that they know something of the anatomy. She suggests that this sort of enlightened experience would eradicate the situation illustrated by the boy who drew a picture of his mother with her breasts on her back. Greengross advocates the use of plaster models as a reasonable substitute: for instance, a girl who cannot see photographs of an erect penis may avoid a harrow-ing experience later on if she can feel a model of one.[7]

Expressing basic needs

While levels of dependency vary, some clients and residents must rely heavily on members of staff for many of their basic needs, needs that are discreetly attended to by those living freely in the com-munity without reference to anybody else and in complete anony-mity. At the request of a resident – or a housebound client – how would social workers feel about purchasing not only the easily obtainable packets of condoms and tubes of contraceptive jelly but pornographic magazines, vibrators or a full-size blow-up doll complete with realistic vagina, pubic hair and breasts? If truly a worker is the eyes, arms and legs of a disabled person then the task does not include passing judgement, pushing aside the request with laughter or delaying in the hope that the resident or client will not repeat his request. For the person sitting in a wheelchair or stretched out on a bed for 24 hours each day with money to spend and sexual fantasies as vivid as his or her able-bodied care givers, delayed gratification must cause additional problems. Hence the need, I feel, to be quite clear in our own minds about the sexual rights of handicapped people.

At least one home I know will arrange for the services of a prostitute at the request of a resident, although another insists that the resident himself – provided he has no speech defect – should speak on the telephone after the number has been obtained, that is, if he is unable to dial it himself. I no longer feel that there are moral issues here. The question must be examined solely in the context of the rights of the client who must decide whether or not at any time he wishes to buy sex in this way. And this I state against a background of thousands and thousands of men – at all levels of society, married and unmarried – who visit prostitutes on countless occasions each year. Of course the feelings of other residents have to be considered, but given an appropriate living environment and professional attitudes that respect confidentiality and avoid gossip, it should be possible to respond to such a request from a resident. This approach is in contrast to probably the most wicked piece of 'humour' I have ever heard: a care worker threatening – albeit good naturedly – to stick a pin in the highly-valued well used and some-what battered blow-up doll which stood in the corner of Joe's room. For Joe this was 'his woman', his comfort at night, his aid to the relief of sexual tensions. Never will I forget the cruelty of that threat.

The incident described earlier between John and Ted is a current, pressing issue. I now know through my contacts with staff groups in several homes that physically handicapped residents are mastur-bated by care staff, both males and females, as a far more common occurrence than would be generally believed. It is interesting that women appear able to respond in this way with less embarrassment and anxiety than men. Most often the response is without the knowledge of colleagues although I recently learned of one man being masturbated from time to time by two different members of staff, neither of whom knew about the involvement of the other. Sharing, with some apprehension, in another staff group the fact that she was providing sexual relief for a 30-year-old resident a care giver unexpectedly – but with delight – found that several of her colleagues, including a female member of staff near to retirement age, were acting in the same way, feeling extremely isolated about the 'private arrangements' that had been made. But, of course, there can be problems, and that is why a staff forum is important as a support network. I have some ambivalence here, having previously stated in Chapter 3 that 'sex is a very private affair'. On the other hand, staff do need protection.

One woman told me about Tom who, while repairs were being done to the plumbing in his house and his sister was in hospital, attended a day centre attached to a residential unit. Because of the problems at home arrangements were made for Tom to have a shower in the unit each day. Janice, his care giver, who usually helped him, described what happened:

Almost as soon as he had taken off his clothes Tom would get an erection.

Because of his handicap he found difficulty in reaching his penis and even more difficulty in rubbing himself up. Sometimes he would ejaculate at once, with his penis scarcely being touched. At other times he would push my hand between his legs, telling me to put soap on his prick and balls. Then he was usually able to come quite quickly. I was very pleased when his sister came out of hospital – apparently she used to masturbate him regularly – and Tom didn't have to have his showers in the unit. One day I thought to myself: 'What would my husband say if he knew?' I think that he would have been quite angry and probably said that he didn't want me to go to work to wank other men.

More serious was the problem of 28-year-old Wendy. She had occasionally masturbated a resident in the home in which she worked and undoubtedly the inner tension of the man was consequently reduced in many other areas of his life. When, however, he learned that Wendy was applying for the post of deputy head in another establishment the relationship turned sour and he started to blackmail her, threatening to contact her husband saying that they were having an affair. For Wendy there were several weeks of anxiety, but she decided to call the man's bluff and applied for the post. She was, in fact, the successful applicant and subsequently took up her new appointment. She did, however, keep a link with the man she had helped and eventually he was able to see her without asking to be masturbated. I do not know but my guess is – and Wendy agreed with me – that he had found another member of staff willing to relieve him.

I doubt whether masturbating another person – even as a 'service', without emotional involvement and entirely at the request of that person – can ever be neutral. It may be even more complicated in the case of a severely disabled woman seeking sexual relief, and what feelings are aroused in acting as third party to a couple needing help to achieve penetration? Perhaps it is important to acknowledge any feelings. Denial would be unhealthy and it would seem better sense to note, to oneself or in supervision, the level of stimulation and excitement experienced by the care giver. At the point where he or she is becoming very excited by the act and the care giver has the primary interest in the sexual activity the warning signals should be heeded. And such excitement can and does occur.

For readers wishing to think further about working with the sexuality and sexual needs of physically disabled people a series of advisory leaflets is available, offering help in suggesting different positions for sexual intercourse and pointing to the wide range of sexual aids now available. These include various devices which may help a man to improve a rather limp erection or to prevent a premature ejaculation where this is a problem; ideas about obtaining satisfaction from oral-genital sex; and encouragement to proceed with sexual activities despite difficulties caused by muscular spasms in the legs, dressings or severe scarring.[8]

One area of concern for members of staff keen to enable handicapped people to enjoy as full and appropriate an expression of their sexuality as possible, and this includes both mentally and physically handicapped people, is the way in which the care givers themselves may become the fantasy objects of disabled people. This is obviously a point for consideration when a member of staff is masturbating a resident or assisting in the act. Ruth described how she had approached the task of masturbating a resident in a very matter-of-fact manner but was emotionally shocked at the moment of the man's ejaculation when he explicitly included her in his fantasies, and subsequently 'felt' the power of his gaze variously directed at her breasts, her bottom or her crotch whenever she walked past him. With mentally handicapped people their desires and their fantasies are often verbalised more crudely, and are therefore easier to process, but in the case of an intelligent, attractive physically disabled person the verbalised fantasies have more serious connotations and implications.

Even within established relationships staff and management anxieties abound, fears about sexual activities colouring attitudes towards other aspects of the caring task. In one home for physically handicapped adults a member of staff, Jeanne, has become engaged to one of the residents, Mike. This relationship has generally been welcomed, but the senior staff of the home have decided that, now Mike is her fiancé, it is no longer right for Jeanne to give Mike his urine bottle nor to help him to have a bath. She was, of course, doing both these jobs before the couple became engaged. So Mike has to ask other staff for his bottle while Jeanne stands alongside. Strange indeed! Jeanne will no doubt take over again when the couple marry later in the year.

Sex and mentally handicapped people

In moving to a consideration of mentally handicapped people, many of the same problems and negative attitudes are presently found, with the weight of public prejudice probably even heavier. Many people are still repulsed by the idea that mentally handicapped people have a right to a sexual life. It seems important, therefore, to explode a number of myths: (i) that the sexual development of many handicapped children, young people and adults varies a great deal from parallel growth in the rest of the population; (ii) that most people regarded as mentally handicapped give cause for complaints about their sexual behaviour; and (iii) that they are more prone to sexual violence than other people. None has any foundation.

The case is clearly stated in a publication entitled *Sexuality and Subnormality*.[9] In adopting a view on sexuality in which the sexual relationship 'can be regarded as something which is valuable, good and satisfying and to be enjoyed in itself' (p. 1) the Swedish authors argue in favour of allowing sexual activity its rightful place in the lives of mentally handicapped people. Naturally this would apply no less to those living in residential settings. With safeguards to protect handicapped people from exploitation and with current contraceptive knowledge there is no reason to become apprehensive about the development of heterosexual relationships among mentally handicapped people. Homosexual relationships, too, will develop. Not all relationships will have a physical base but, if this happens: 'Today one cannot any longer disregard the mentally handicapped person's right to the rewards and satisfactions of a sex life' (p. 4). There will be problems as in other expressive and developmental phases. However, in counteracting the loneliness so acutely felt by many mentally handicapped people and in the total life enrichment process of residents to which social workers must be committed, the question of rights and duties must be squarely faced. The authors of *Sexuality and Subnormality* further argue that many handicapped people are able to sustain satisfying sexual relationships, thereby lessening the states of tension in which they exist. We are reminded that a mentally handicapped couple, with or without a child, can find happiness in marriage and live together like other human beings who are fond of each other. These marriages can work out just as well, or as badly, as any other marriage (p. 20).

In practice, difficulties still exist for mentally handicapped people. Their families are often over-protective, and the external managers of residential homes seem all too rarely able to make a stand on behalf of the staffs of their homes trying to work to professional standards in bureaucratic organisations willing to put their 'public image' before the needs and rights of residents.

I am aware that masturbation does sometimes present a problem to staff working with mentally handicapped people, especially adolescents and young adults. The answer does not lie, as I heard recently, in giving the young man a tissue, a look of disgust and instructions to go to the toilet. For mentally handicapped people, learning to masturbate in private, or with a chosen partner, is a social skill to be learned like any other on the list of acceptable practices and customs which non-handicapped people acquire in the course of growing up without too much direct instruction. Green-gross gives a delightful example of the response to a boy living in his own home:

> The mother of a handicapped child told me of the first time she 'caught', to use her own words, her son masturbating. She was horrified and ran to her husband. He told her quietly to turn her back 'because her son was learning a skill'. He suggested that her only involvement be making sure the boy could reach for the paper tissues to clean up after him so that parents need not be involved. [10]

What appears to be happening now in many residential homes is that, with or without the knowledge and agreement of external managers, staff – often enthusiastic through training – are crashing through the old taboos and facilitating the sexual expression of residents where appropriate with sensitivity and professional wisdom by rearranging the accommodation in living units, ordering double beds and working in some depth with residents about the management of their sexual needs. I have been heartened of late by what I have heard, and seen, in a number of residential homes and hostels. Sadly, I know that staff groups in other establishments are a long way behind in their ideas, unaware of the new spirit of adventurous caring. When I pause and think of perhaps 30 adults – who happen to be mentally handicapped – spending most of their time together in the same residential establishment yet destined to live out their lives without sharing a comfortable and right-sized bed, if they so wish, with a partner of the same or the opposite sex solely on account of the poor design of the physical structure of the building; the prejudices of elected members or senior managers; and the fears of care staff and their immediate line managers, I ask myself what sort of care givers they have. Fortunately, as I said, other staff groups are exclusively client-centred, basing their practice on the need to improve the residents' life experiences and levels of satisfaction.

The recent publication by MIND on sex and social expression for mentally handicapped people, called *Getting Together*, [11] is a most encouraging statement for those working seriously with this client group. A number of important points are made in the document, for

example: (i) given that government policy is for mentally handicapped people to live as normally as possible, it is curious to observe
that the law continues effectively to prohibit *any* sexual relationships between severely mentally handicapped people; (ii) despite
the current restrictions of the criminal law, there is plenty of scope
for improving the quality of life for mentally handicapped people;
(iii) MIND's view is that those people who wish to enter into a full
sexual relationship and perhaps to marry and have children should
not be hindered by the obstacles posed by dismissive and un-
enlightened attitudes; and (iv) as long as members of staff act
reasonably, it is unlikely that a civil action would be brought against
them for encouraging sexual relationships to develop between their
patients or clients. As the report rightly concludes, however:

> . . . clarification of the civil law and a memorandum of guidance from the
> DHSS is urgently needed in order to remove the inhibitions felt by many
> staff. MIND strongly believes that the initiative begun by staff working
> with mentally handicapped people in hospitals, residential centres and
> the community should be supported and developed to enable those in
> their care to lead as emotionally full and 'normal' a life as possible. (p. 18)

Homosexual relationships

So far the principal consideration in this chapter has been heterosexual relationships. Since one in 20 of the population is thought to
be homosexual or to be inclined towards homosexuality, then it
follows that among handicapped people there will be some homosexuals.[12] It would appear that for a long while they will remain one
of the most stigmatised groups. As a friend said to me recently, 'A
disabled gay really is at the bottom of the pile.' I bring in this
question of homosexuality at this point because it highlights the
special needs of a special group of staff, namely, those who are
homosexual. Until we are able to accommodate them fully and
without prejudice into our staff groups, and to make the best use of
their special feelings and special knowledge both as people and as
counsellors, then the outlook for homosexual residents must indeed
be bleak. And some local authorities and voluntary organisations
retain the entrenched positions of a different era. As a result of this
the social work profession has itself been compromised by events in
1981 and 1982: that staff can be dismissed because of their sexual
orientation. I think, therefore, that we should keep alive the issues
raised by the cases of Susan Shell and Judith Williams.

Susan Shell, a 31-year-old residential social worker, was sus-
pended from her job at a hostel for adolescent girls after it had been

reported, on her own admission, that she was a lesbian. The management decision was upheld by a tribunal drawn from members of the council's establishment committee and Susan Shell was dismissed, solely, it would appear, because of her sexual orientation. Her work was satisfactory in every respect.

According to the press,[13] the local authority made some extremely weak responses to the union official representing Susan Shell. For example, it was stated that it is the responsibility of social services departments to encourage the socio–sexual norms of marriage and children in the young people in their care, and it was not prepared to debate the philosophy of homosexuality. Furthermore, the union official could elicit no comment when he asked whether a member of staff of ten years' standing would be sacked if he or she decided to 'come out'.

I wonder how secure other gay social workers in that particular social services department, field and residential, now feel, for instance, when faced with social work supervision. Surely it must be reduced to a bizarre game with a potentially vast area of the practitioner's work, that is, anything connected with the sexuality of clients or residents, necessarily avoided to protect the worker from having to declare his or her hand.

What message did the girls in the hostel receive as a result of Susan Shell's dismissal, especially any 16-year-old who is perhaps just realising that she is a lesbian? Her worry may be that if the fact becomes known she will lose her job. For many girls the socio–sexual norms of marriage and children are undoubtedly to be encouraged. My concern is about our attitudes towards those who do not choose this path, who intentionally or unintentionally have children without marriage, or who by the time they leave care at 18 years of age are certain of their homosexual orientation.

If in a local authority there is unwillingness even to debate the philosophy of homosexuality can we be sure that everything possible is done for young people in care who may be homosexual, not only by lessening the feelings of stigma and unhealthy difference perpetuated by the man in the street, but by enabling them to accept and eventually to enjoy their sexual orientation? This may sometimes be one of the social work tasks with a young person in residential care, but undertaken with difficulty if, in other establishments in the department, staff members are being dismissed for being gay. If such cavalier treatment is permissible without an allegation, what level of confidence can there be about obtaining a 'fair hearing' when a report is made about a sexual encounter between a resident and a staff member?

Social workers in senior positions should surely demonstrate consistently their understa !xing of the human condition, of the nature of sexuality, and of the way sexual orientation is determined or decided upon. Too many people deny homosexuality or reject it blindly. Writing about the dismissal of Susan Shell Alan Webster stated:

> I believe that for too long we have soft pedalled, tried to ignore, or simply swept under the carpet the question of homosexuality. The Bible quite firmly states that homosexuality is perverse and against the order of things as created by Almighty God, and is therefore most definitely wrong.[14]

We do not perhaps worship the same God. Mine is much more tolerant, filled with understanding and compassion, looking not at some notion of perversity, not at whether a woman chooses to sleep with a man or another woman, but at the quality of the exchanges, wherever they may occur. The case of Susan Shell was followed in 1982 by that of Judith Williams who was dismissed from her post in a voluntary home for disturbed adolescent girls. As reported in the social work journals[15] the issues appeared more complex with her employers maintaining that the dismissal was because the worker was 'temperamentally unsuitable'. Others, however, saw the action of the agency as a flagrant example of discrimination, particularly in the knowledge of its general policy on the employment of staff: 'Such persons should be mature, stable adults who identify with the conventional adult model normally accepted by society.' And at that home, too, there must be young people wanting reassurance that it is 'OK to be gay'.

Fortunately there are other models to be found. A friend of mine worked first as a residential social worker and then as a teacher. As she grew through late adolescence to womanhood she gave every appearance of being heterosexual in the nature and conduct of her relationships with both men and women. In the children's home where I knew her best she was an excellent worker, made easy contact with children and young people, responded with skill and sensitivity to their needs and fought doggedly on their behalf whenever she felt that short cuts were being taken with good child care practice. I was fond of Carol and appreciated her talents and human qualities.

In the third year of teacher training it became apparent that she was a lesbian. After a number of comparatively brief involvements with women of her own age, akin to many traditional heterosexual courting rituals, Carol settled down in a steady partnership which has lasted for several years. In her own estimation she is now a 'married woman'. Carol is again employed in a social work agency, working with young people for part of the time, and she makes no effort to hide the fact that she is gay.

It worries me that had Carol applied for a residential social work post in the local authority from which Susan Shell was dismissed, and had she declared her lesbianism, she might not have been accepted for the job. Had she remained silent but later been 'found out' she might swiftly have become yet another victim of fears, fantasies and prejudice. As it is, she is at present judged by her work performance, and her sexual orientation, for those to whom it is important, is a secondary consideration. She has the highest personal and professional standards and, with additional experience, works even more effectively than nine years ago when I believed her to be heterosexual. As a colleague I would still feel as safe with Carol as ever before.

I cannot comment further about Judith Williams, but the fact that she received massive union support must speak for itself. I am certain, however, that Susan Shell had a contribution to make – if only she had been given the chance. However, for many people, rejection provides the most comfortable escape because they then do not have to confront the latent homosexuality within themselves. For this reason, sometimes those who should be our colleagues become victims as easily as do residents.

Such management decisions – as in the case of Susan Shell – and such policy statements – as in the case of Judith Williams – must put on edge any member of staff who may be homosexual or, indeed, those called upon to work intimately with clients or residents, and particularly those involved with children and young people where allegations are most likely. If this happens to female members of staff how much more likely is it to occur with males? How does it affect the work that is necessary and possible with the whole range of client groups mentioned in this chapter when the primary concern of the worker must be personal safety, knowing that the employing authority is fearful even of appointing members of staff who are homosexual? A chapter on special needs and special groups must, therefore, consider this very special staff group. The attitudes of management towards them have a direct bearing on the care standards it is possible to provide for clients.

In concluding this chapter it seems right to return to the needs of residents. And some of these may be lesbians. The head of a home for physically handicapped people described to me the problems in dressing a 21-year-old lesbian. Each morning Fiona clings tightly to the female member of staff who is assisting her, endeavouring to keep their breasts squeezed together for as long as possible. Fiona has in the past been made to feel very guilty by some members of staff who seem out of touch with the young woman's intense emotions. Fortunately, there is a lesbian on the staff who is able to discuss with Fiona many aspects of her sexuality, and to give her genuine confirmation that her thoughts and desires are healthy and merit respect.

Handicapped people are among the minority groups in this country. Homosexuals are also included in these minorities. As a sexual being with disability of body or mind living in a residential unit and dependent upon other people for many essentials of every-day existence, the opportunities for the expression of sexual needs may undoubtedly be precarious. If your sexual orientation inclines you towards physical contact and intimacy with members of the same sex, then very special support and understanding will be required. This 'very special support and understanding' is not to help the resident to 'come to terms with' a disability and to bring him or her to a position of self-acceptance as an asexual person, but rather to find ways in which his or her sexuality can find its rightful place in daily living. Different people, with different sexual orientations, may be able to help in this search.

5 Sexual Encounters Between Adults and Children

Social workers bring to any case arising from sexual encounters between adults and children – 'sexual abuse' in common parlance – the complexity derived from their personal and professional sexual selves. The moral, social and philosophical questions about the nature of sexuality are, in this area of practice, among the most fundamental they are called to unravel. Despite such complexity and the diversity to be found among any group of social workers there is potential for the healthy resolution of even the most worrying problems. Given adequate levels of support and social work supervision, and time to work on their cases, practitioners can often help individuals troubled and traumatized by sexual abuse – and their families, too – to reaffirm positive elements of their social, sexual and emotional selves: by the sensitivity of their approach; by their overall analysis and assessment; by their determination to lessen the pathological connotations of such sexual activity; and by their ability to hold within an emotional framework all the fine strands of feeling which go towards the make-up of those involved before, during and after – sometimes long after – incidents have occurred.

When working with sexually abused children and their families social workers will frequently be involved with both victims and offenders in a way not always understood or accepted by other professional groups with different goals, different tasks and different perspectives. Teachers, lawyers and even health visitors may sometimes disagree with social workers. While ostensibly impartial, the police are ultimately concerned with findings of 'innocence' or 'guilt', and with ensuring that offenders against the law appear before the courts. They may be over-zealous on occasions in their attempts to bring about convictions. At other times they may be limited in their compassion and sensitivity in questioning victims and offenders. They may be less than tolerant with those who already have convictions, with people who live in residential homes and hostels or with those who have previously come to their notice in other connections.

There is a wide range of cases which currently come under the heading of sexual abuse, both inside and outside the family. Social workers may become involved at any stage. Sometimes they will be applying their knowledge, skill and understanding to the most vicious and vile incidents with children and here there will usually be a large measure of agreement with social work colleagues and with those from other interested disciplines. Jane is now 14 years of age and, although partly erased by time, an incident of four years ago continues to colour aspects of her life. When she was 10 she was taken to the shed in her garden by a young man known to her family and sexually abused. He kept her there for several hours against her will and urinated in her mouth. Jane was lucky to escape with her life, and few would disagree with the need for the assailant to be removed from the community. There may, however, be considerable debate about the nature and extent of the punishment or the treatment he should receive.

Fortunately, the majority of sexual abuse cases with which social workers are involved – whether incestuous or not – while making an emotional and physical assault upon the child, do not put him or her at risk of bodily injury. Sometimes, when working with young people, social workers may need to question the very term 'sexual abuse', deciding whether their response to a problem is best approached from a position which admits no other possibility. Social workers will most frequently be working in grey areas where the sexual element of the contact between the adult and the child is sometimes less easily categorised as an offence against the law, where the moral issues are less pronounced and where the most damaging experience may be the clumsy professional intervention or the exaggerated reactions of family, friends, neighbours or teachers. One girl I worked with, some would say a girl at risk, was subjected at home to a barrage of innuendo and comparatively minor physical molestation. Her step-father – with whom she maintained a friendly relationship – always insisted on changing his clothes in the living room in her presence, would forever be making remarks about the shape of her bottom and as part of his boisterous, sexually provocative play with younger children in the family would suggest to the three-year-old that he should go and fondle Donna's breasts 'to see how they are growing'. Fortunately, Donna, at 14 years of age, had well-developed social skills, a confidence with adults and the level of understanding of a much older girl. She used her maturity to respond quite coldly to these assaults upon her increasingly obvious adolescent sexuality while keeping her place within the family, a family that was extremely important to her.

Unresolved conflicts

I work part time as a consultant in residential care in a number of community homes, both with staff groups and with groups of staff and young people, and was for several years myself a residential social worker. Not infrequently the personal histories of the children and young people in residential centres contain reports of sexual abuse, sometimes closely related to their reception into care. The later behaviour of other children and young people in residential settings may indicate sexual awareness beyond their years and establish the fact that they, too, have witnessed or been engaged in sexual activities with adults likely to be psychologically disturbing. In the same residential setting may be living other young adults of 15, 16 or 17 who themselves have sexually abused children.

As grown-ups, people may wrestle for years with unresolved conflicts arising from sexual experiences with an adult during their childhood or adolescence. Those labelled as offenders, criminals or perverts are also, in most instances, not without very strong feelings and have to go on living and breathing; developing; interacting and communicating; and contributing to a world in which they have to make relationships in order to survive.

Case examples

I am thinking particularly of a number of cases with which I have been concerned, involving a range of people, both young and old, and offer them as illustrations. These must, of course, be thumbnail sketches stripped of their contexts and nuances, but are sufficient to show the networks that are affected and the possible ramifications arising from sexual contacts with children and young people initiated by adults. The first is about two little girls, *Sharon* and *Sheila*, aged three and five years respectively, admitted to residential care following the desertion of their mother and the inability of their father to look after them single-handed during the week. In their play activities with other youngsters in the home they were soon seen quite openly to be suggesting sexual games and simulating intercourse. The reply to staff endeavouring to divert the group was: 'Daddy used to play with us like this.' The evidence against the girls' father was insufficient for anything to be proved, but a voluntary arrangement was made for Sharon and Sheila to be cared for by their grandparents on their weekend visits home. That there was a strong bond of affection between this man and his children I could be in no doubt; that the children were at risk in the coming years I was equally certain; and that the family could only be worked with in the climate of a trusting relationship had to be the basis of professional intervention. Eventually, and without convicting himself, the girls' father came as near as possible to saying that he had become sexually aroused as a result of physical contact with his young daughters, that he had initiated play with them that caused excitement and gave satisfaction, and that his sexual interest in Sharon and Sheila only started after his wife had started to refuse him sexual intercourse. In starting a new relationship with a girl from his place of work the sexual interest in his daughters certainly seemed to lessen – he became much less anxious and more fatherly – but uncertainty remained about the reasons for his wife's departure and the real order of events.

Keith was 14 years of age when admitted to residential care. He had had an unhealthy relationship with his mother since his father's death six years previously. He had always slept with her and there was impenetrable emotional interdependence. Keith's disturbance was first noticed at school and a referral was made to the social services department, his mother's unexpected admission to hospital almost immediately necessitating the boy's move away from his own home. Within six months of Keith's reception into care the young residential social worker temporarily in charge of the group in which the boy lived was forced to resign his post following allegations of a sexual relationship between him and Keith. Other reports highlighted Keith's sexual activities with boys of his own age living in the unit. I accept that the onus was on the residential social worker to avoid such involvement, however inexperienced, naïve and unsophisticated he may have been and however poor the quality of the agency support systems necessary for him to work in a professional way, but there is no doubt in my mind that Keith's heightened awareness, his detailed knowledge of sexual activities and his particular stage of adolescent development combined to give him unnatural powers of seduction *vis-à-vis* the young worker compelled to hand in his resignation.

I am aware that this theory of seduction by adolescents is not universally accepted, but I offer it as one factor that social workers must be aware of in their efforts to understand problems in the round. Before reaching 15 years of age, Keith had already been his mother's lover and had experienced his sexuality as sufficiently powerful to destroy the career of a promising, sensitive worker. I know that Keith felt bad about the outcome of his relationship with his care giver – he was not an angry, aggressive boy – and was genuinely fond of one of the very few adult males who had ever entered his life. Sadly for Keith, relationships, inside or outside the family, with same-age or older partners, had come to include sexual activity.

In discussion about Keith it has been suggested to me that it is reasonable to suppose that a deeply loving and sustained relationship with a man, whether or not sex was part of it, was the one way that Keith's symbiotic maternal tie could have been broken without severe emotional damage. I agree about the relationship, and while I am not convinced by the arguments for a sexual relationship with a man given the boy's age, I would point out that in reacting to sexual encounters between adults and children in which those involved may, in the first instance, appear to be appropriately categorised as offenders and victims social workers should consider any differences of approach when the exchanges have been reciprocally desired and reciprocally enjoyed. Such relationships are not all that uncommon. Most frequently social workers will choose to set aside this element of reciprocity but undoubtedly the line between victims and offenders becomes more blurred as a child moves into young adulthood, and two relevant examples are given at the end of the next chapter.

We can learn a great deal from literature and Keith always reminds me of Paul in *Sons and Lovers*.[1] Paul, too, may have slept with his mother on occasion and as the story unfolds we learn of this young man's later difficulties in his relationships with women, namely Miriam and Clara. Paul, I feel, was always uncertain of his sexual identity, was a mixture of tenderness and harshness, had strong sexual feelings, yet was bound by his own virginity when presented with the opportunity for adult sexual exchanges. For Paul the movement from a symbiotic relationship with his mother to a later diatrophic relationship became an impossibility, and I have often wondered about readers' reactions to Paul had he broken out of his virginity by engaging in a sexual relationship with younger members of the family or a neighbour's child. Both, to my mind, were possibilities given his psychological development and his relationship with his mother.

Keith became a problem to himself, and to others, throughout his stay in care. Members of staff were naturally wary of physical contact with him yet he desperately needed it; he seemed unable to become excited by relationships with any of the girls who admired his athletic skills and enjoyed his company; he appeared sexually attracted to younger boys in the unit; and all but rejected his mother when her new boyfriend, a nurse from the hospital where she was a patient for nearly a year, moved in. In retrospect, I believe that there was time between the ages of 15 and 18 when it would have been possible to work intensively with Keith on the difficulties he had grown up with. But, for whatever reason, this was not done. In practice, and as a further illustration of some of the themes developed in Chapter 2, this shows how even young people who have come into care for reasons of a sexual origin – either as victims or offenders – are perhaps rarely given the opportunity to 'talk sex' in a manner which will allow them to explore in a safe environment their past experiences, to make some sense of their sexual orientation, whether temporary or permanent, and to be helped to feel comfortable with it.

My next two examples relate to adolescent girls, 15 years of age, both of whom had sexual intercourse with their fathers over a period of two or three years. *Susan* came from what seemed to be a stable, caring, lively family and moved into residential care at the point of investigations and before her father was committed to prison, the man having gone to the police of his own accord to make a statement regarding his incestuous relationship with his daughter. The girl continued to love her father, was deeply affected by his imprisonment and, for a long while, was tortured by her own guilt and the memory of her willingness to participate in sexual activities which culminated so disastrously for her father and for the family. Towards the end of the two-year period during which her father was imprisoned, Susan found a boyfriend and was four months pregnant by the time her father was released. She delayed marriage until he was free to attend the ceremony and thus made her own practical – and, I think, emotional – arrangements for not having to risk a repetition of past events while maintaining her links with the family. With Susan living away from the parental home it was possible for her mother, with social work support, to rekindle the relationship that had once existed between her and her husband.

Much less certainty surrounded *Moira's* allegations of an incestuous relationship with her father in a family renowned for its problems, its intrigues and – dare I say? – its deviousness. Certainly the members of the family were familiar with the power of blackmail in getting their own way, and for some time Moira's allegations seemed part of this pattern. The girl's father was a good-natured man in ill health and frequently drunk. Thinking back it may well be that I liked him too much to believe his daughter's tales until on one occasion at midnight, accompanied by a policeman, I called at Moira's family flat in an attempt to find her after she had failed to return from a supposedly strictly-controlled home visit on a day away from the residential unit where she was living. We found Moira in bed with her father. In the event, the man died before police investigations were completed.

Adult recollections

As I mentioned earlier, many adults contain within them very powerfully any illicit exchanges they experienced as children, either with related or non-related adults. Equally powerful in their inner worlds are their recollections of the reactions of family and friends at the moment of discovery. It is not inevitable that people will be troubled later in life – and current awareness of the high incidence of sexual abuse would confirm this[2] – and I have spoken to many adults, sexually and socially mature adults, who on their own or with the help of a friend or family or professional worker have overcome or been able to set aside successfully childhood incidents. The need for a professional response at the time of disclosure and investigation is a point that will be developed later in the chapter.

For some people, however, the memory of incidents of sexual abuse may remain dormant year after year. On a short course for social workers we were focusing on the topic of feelings and emotions, and particularly on the feelings raised in us by adults accused of sexual interference with children or young people. One member of the group, a 40-year-old woman in charge of a community home, revealed for the first time in her life an experience with her male piano teacher when she was 12 years of age. She spoke of her terror after the indecent act, of her flight from his home, of her need to regain her composure before she reached her own home because of the strained relationships she already experienced there, and of her struggle to invent stories in order never to have to take piano lessons with that teacher again.

On a similar course looking at questions of adolescent sexuality another woman of about the same age, 40 years, the intensity of her feelings understandably aroused by the subject under discussion, asked to see me privately at the end of the seminar. In a later intensive counselling session she described how only at that stage of her life – and indeed as a result of some of the free exchanges that had taken place among group members – was she able to tell anybody of the incestuous relationship which for so many years she had both endured and enjoyed with her father prior to his death when she was 22 years of age. Sexually, and to an extent socially, she had been handicapped ever since, not easily making relationships with either males or females of her own age, yet somehow able to give primary care to groups of young children in a day centre where she worked. The feelings of this woman were mixed, but basically she was angry with a father who, as she saw it, had at one and the same time cheated her during her developmental years and subsequently by his untimely death at 48 years of age.

Emotional complexity
Sexual exchanges are never neutral. Sexual exchanges between adults and children or young people, and especially between members of the same family, are charged with an emotional force rarely experienced elsewhere: a mixture of fear, contentment, anger, excitement and guilt, usually bounded by a desperate need on the part of one or both participants to keep secret the nature of the relationship. While in the eyes of the man in the street, the police and the judiciary, the responsibility is most frequently seen to lie firmly with the adult, the young partner – the young victim – may not always, as we have seen, make such a clear division as the investigating officials between the victim and the offender. This is especially true with adolescents who may wince in the knowledge of the subsequent distress, shame, humiliation and incarceration of the adults with whom they have had a sexual liaison. Adolescent perspectives may change as they leave their formative years and understanding and interpretation of events may shift over time, but many are deeply conscious of their own part in the physical and emotional exchanges.

   The complexity and long-lasting effects of incestuous relationships may ripple through the whole family many years after the incident in ways perhaps not always expected. A friend of mine, attached to the outpatients' department of a large psychiatric unit, has been working with a Turkish woman who is experiencing alienation from her husband, sensing that he has rapidly moved away from her emotionally and now pays excessive attention to their daughter. The client herself makes a link between her current feelings of rejection and earlier family experiences. Her own father had incestuous relationships with her two sisters during their adolescence, but had never touched her in a sexual way. Her reaction was not one of relief as many would expect. For many years she had been preoccupied with wanting to know why she had never been sufficiently attractive to her father for him to want a sexual relationship with her.

   Earlier I mentioned prison when referring to Susan's incestuous relationship with her father. On the other side of the wall, as it were, I recall working in prison with a man who prior to committal was a farm labourer living with his wife and four daughters in a remote rural area. He had had sexual relations with three of the girls, two of whom had become pregnant. He had a rough time in prison, each piece of news that filtered through to him – for example, about his wife's losing battle to retain the tied cottage in which they had lived since their marriage, about the possible break-up of the family, and about the illness and subsequent death of his own parents destroyed by their son's imprisonment – striking blow after blow to the emotional and mental fabric of a man already ageing five years in one as a result of the unprecedented pressures on his physical being. As wrong as this man's behaviour had been, there was a reciprocal bond of affection between him and his wife and his children, the punishment he received settling indiscriminately like nuclear fall-out on all members of the family. That, unfortunately, is the catastrophic effect of many of our responses to sexual activities which breach the code of conduct we have established within our society. Most often the emotional future of one party is tied to the emotional future of the other, regardless of the victim and offender labels attached by various legal, lay and professional groups.

A former student of mine described to me what he had seen on placement in a large prison. In the reception area where new clothing was issued he witnessed the admission of a Rule 43 prisoner, that is, one who for his own safety is segregated from other inmates. The man who was being admitted had been convicted following the discovery of his sexual involvement with his step-daughter and his niece. Other prisoners working in the clothing store made it their business to check his card giving brief personal details and they learned the nature of the offence. Within half an hour, and before having the opportunity to be locked in a cell on his own, the man had been beaten up, kicked about his body and particularly about his testicles. For the duration of his sentence he was destined to live in fear.

The social work task
For the social worker, the task of analysing, understanding, repairing and healing is one which often extends over several years; it is one which may only begin in earnest when the investigations are complete, when the parties are separated, when a decision has been made whether or not to prosecute or when the verdict of the court has been announced; it is one which may need addressing and

readdressing at different points and with different sorts of intervention throughout the lives of those involved, whether, as I suggested, as victims or offenders. It is my experience that, where the outcome for at least one party is traumatic and visible, there are few people who are able to lay to rest without intra-personal conflict the ghosts of a sexual experience in childhood. And, as we have seen, even when the incidents or episodes are initially resolved by the individuals concerned without external intervention, the residual feelings may fade only on the surface. There is no doubt that in children and young people these feelings may stem directly from the breakdown in trust which they were entitled to rely upon as members of a family or as young people in the care of non-related adults. Sometimes, I would contend, they stem from the policies and practices which society has adopted as the appropriate responses to reports of sexual encounters between adults and children, and sometimes from gauche handling of individual cases. Both the former and the latter may cause even more emotional bruising to the identified victim, bringing about his or her rejection from the family group; and alienating and depressing the identified offender to such an extent that chances of rehabilitation become minimal.

That is why, in my opinion, the dilemmas facing the social worker are particularly acute at five stages in the process of intervention: (i) suspicion and confrontation; (ii) accusation of or confession by an adult, or the report of an incident by a child or young person; (iii) the investigation; (iv) police involvement and possible court proceedings; and (v) the aftermath. Sometimes, from my experience, signals may be given to future clients – by social workers or other people – and paths laid down which will make more difficult, or even impossible, the essential work to be tackled.

Because of their close contact with individuals and families, in both field and residential settings, social workers are able to pick up from clients a host of cues about possible involvement in sexual abuse: by the moods they observe, by the words they hear and by the feelings that are expressed. The point at which they help a woman to talk about the incestuous relationship between her husband and her daughter or the sexual play between her lodger and her son; or a young person to talk about a sexual relationship with an adult is important. Different times and different circumstances will bring forth a denial or a willingness to share everything in detail. Having received information, the social worker has to decide what to do with it. As I stated earlier, the social worker often works in grey areas, weighing up what is lawful, what is unlawful, what is only just unlawful and what is unlawful but, in the worker's opinion, not damaging to the client. Most young people are aware of the power of their sexuality, both inside and outside the family. The social worker must respond in a way that neither shows disbelief nor condemns an adult out of hand. The worker seeks clarification and meaning, needing to give context to incident and episode. At the point of investigation he or she must think of the future, about the need to work purposefully at a later date with someone who may see him or her initially as a police officer in plain clothes. In court proceedings, too, there is need to be aware of the way evidence is presented and of the effect on individuals of a court appearance in which the most intimate details of their sexual conduct may be made public. Immediately afterwards, with the whole family together again or with one member missing; with trauma present from whatever source, social workers have to assist those involved in keeping some sort of perspective. Children and adults may now view each other differently, they may have a strange new awareness of having broken or been accused of breaking one of the strongest taboos in our society, and they will have a redefined image of themselves as sexual beings.

Both inside and outside the family changing patterns of behaviour within an overt close relationship between an adult and a child or young person may give an indication of a sexual relationship: secrecy or secret meetings; embarrassment of the adult in discussing the child or young person; inappropriate expensive gifts; unexplained sums of money in the possession of the child or young person; over-possessiveness on the part of the adult; excessive curiosity or embarrassment about sex on the part of the child or young person; unwillingness by the adult to allow the child or young person to mix naturally with peers; a poor self-image in the child or young person; altered sleep patterns; unexplained withdrawal from school activities; and a variety of physical symptoms, particularly in younger children, for example, hyperactivity, a reoccurrence of bed-wetting or compulsive masturbation.

And, then, for the social worker, the greatest dilemma of all: how to cope with the outcome of what has been revealed either by the client or somebody else; how to cope with the unexpected turn of events arising from some revelations for which he or she must take some responsibility; and how to contain the feelings both within himself or herself and within those with whom he or she has worked

– when other forces and other agencies with greater powers and a clear-cut brief do not appear to have the same range of concerns.

Because of my own approach to practice – indeed the combination of all the factors I mentioned at the beginning of Chapter 1 – I have been privileged, particularly in residential work, to get to know as people, and I stress the word 'people', children, adolescents and adults who, in one way or another, have been labelled as victims or offenders, or both. One of the main tasks when working with children and young people sexually abused by adults is to enable them to experience satisfying and satisfactory contact with adults which does not culminate in sexual interference. And, reiterating earlier comments about children's needs for healthy touch experience, this must include physical contact. Knowing that all children – sexually abused or not – need a great deal of affection, cuddles and kisses if they are to grow up with any real hope of successfully parenting their own children, residential social workers are presented with a particular difficulty when giving 24-hours-a-day, seven-days-a-week care to those in their residential homes and schools. My earlier example about the young worker who cared for Keith demonstrated how disastrous the results can be.

A personal experience
In bringing this chapter to a conclusion I am going to recount a very personal experience. I recall working in a residential setting for nearly two years with Linda, a mature and attractive West Indian girl who was 14 years of age at the time of the incident I am describing. Sent to England from the West Indies by her grandparents when she was 10 years old and rejected by her family after evidence of sexual abuse by her step-father in this country, Linda went through a period of great stress and painful isolation from both adults and other children. Beneath her depression could be seen warmth, intelligence and a tremendous capacity to love and be loved. I had had a great deal to do with Linda, often intervening in her moments of greatest despair and alienation from the group and, having lived and worked with her for so long, was very fond of her. She was especially troubled at night and on one occasion sent a message via the member of staff on night duty asking to speak to me. I saw her shortly afterwards. We had a ten-minute conversation from which I realised that Linda was very controlled and ready to settle for the night. Or so I thought. As I went towards the door of the small side room where we had been talking Linda stood up and

slipped off her dressing gown to reveal her brown body clad in the briefest, bikini-type yellow underwear. I remember the moment as one of the most alarming of my career, all life as it were passing before me instantaneously. With a mixture of humour, anxiety and a pretence that I had hardly noticed – although it was obvious that I had – I suggested that it was time for Linda to go to bed, and said that I would ensure that the night staff member on duty brought her a hot drink and a magazine that I would pass on to her. I could so easily have rejected her completely at that moment, and undone all that had been achieved with the girl during her stay with us.

In classical terms Linda had fantasised about the worker as her lover, and was offering herself in gratitude for all the help she felt she had received from me. Had I responded, had the incident become known, and had I been punished in some way, justice would have been seen to have been done. I followed through the incident with Linda. We spoke about it the next day, and she was able to put into words what she sought to express with her body. More importantly, Linda spoke freely, for the first time as a young adult, about what she felt and about what she recollected of having been sexually abused by her step-father. As she spoke, it become apparent that the allegations – which at least in part brought about her reception into care – had far more substance than previously realised by either field or residential social workers:

> At first he only used to cuddle me and I liked it. Sometimes in the mornings he was naked and used to get me to climb into his bed and that was all right as well as we used to play about and it was warm. He used to rub his hand all over my bottom and between my legs and sometimes he would get me to rub his prick. A few times he tried to put it inside me but it always hurt so he gave up and he just used to rub it up and down between my legs instead. He was always very gentle and I knew it was wrong but I think my mum got very jealous about all the attention he paid me. I think he really liked me then, my dad, but he always got very edgy if he thought mum was coming back from work. She used to go off early mornings to clean a block of flats.

Linda's relationship with her step-father was important. Had he been imprisoned – a real possibility if the extent of his physical exchanges with Linda had been known at the time – the whole family may have broken up, and Linda would have been bowed down with guilt. Linda and I still remained close after the incident in the community home and, for Linda, the discussion was a real stage in her development. Certainly I learned a great deal. Now in her twenties, Linda is happily married, and has a successful career. After nearly 15 years of hard work both on her part and on the part of her parents, she has a cordial relationship with her mother, step-father, brother and sister.

Alternative responses

If social workers are, thankfully, only rarely caught up in an incident in the way that I was, they are always in a privileged position *vis-à-vis* the sexual sides of their clients' lives: they have comparatively free access to people's home and will often witness a family act and interact in a way not usually viewed by outsiders; they are often the recipients of very delicate information about the intimacies of people's lives, information sometimes volunteered in desperation in moments of stress or anger; and, as residential social workers, they have responsibilities for both the physical and emotional care of residents, seeing the most vulnerable aspects of their sexual selves.

I am as horrified as anyone else by the sexual abuse of children or young people where the violence of the incident leaves physical damage. I am as aware as anybody else of the psychological damage that may occur following early sexual experience initiated by adults who have abused their positions of power and authority, within or outside the family. As a social worker I am concerned about the immediate and long-term effects of over-reaction in cases of non-violent sexual exchanges and would support any moves from what I still perceive in too many instances as inappropriate responses. Our knowledge is as yet rudimentary. Our response is as yet blunt. Incestuous relationships and sexual encounters between adults and children outside the family have been part of the human condition throughout the centuries. I see no hope of stopping it, lessening it, curing it. Indications are that in the sexually oriented and sexually provocative society we have created, such activities are on the increase. While punishment may be a partial solution, we must consider as a first step a range of alternative responses on the lines of what would appear some of the best work in the United States.[2]

Molesting adults do come out of prison; molested children do remain members of families, even when one of their number is in prison or they themselves are in residential care; molested children grow up, either to become parents themselves, or to carry with them year after year the guilt, uncertainty and confusion arising from the sexual interference, and perhaps compounded by the reactions of those who surrounded them at the time of the incident.

6 Residential Care: Allegations and Responses

There is probably no group of people more dejected than social workers faced with charges of indecent assault. And these more often than not are residential practitioners. Any allegation against a worker – usually followed by suspension and investigation, and sometimes an appearance in court – bites deeply into the very core of that individual's being and, whatever the outcome, he or she will never be the same again. It can happen to almost anybody at any time. It does happen with far greater frequency than is generally known. Most local authorities and voluntary organisations have a number of incidents each year.

Alongside the distress of the accused person may be seen the acute embarrassment of the managers inside or outside the home and the tendency towards 'distance', alienation and the justification for limiting communication to the written word after an initial interview. In my view this is one of the aspects of their work most clumsily dealt with by the external managers of residential homes in some agencies, their deep-seated fears quickly changing to aggression and unspoken reprobation. Elsewhere I described part of a role-play of such an event in which the head of home was himself under suspicion:

> The members of the group played out the incident as administrators, homes advisers and 'duty' fieldworkers from firm desk positions placed around the edge of the room (with much telephoning, uneasy laughter and character smearing) whilst the main subjects remained stunned and unattended on the open floor space. He who five minutes earlier had been a friend and colleague had suddenly become a different kind of being.[1]

An incident of this sort soon becomes *sub judice* in staff meetings yet is a focus of gossip and innuendo. The 'scandal' may be discussed in the neighbourhood or eventually find its way into local or national newspapers. It will hold a particular interest if youngsters are seemingly involved. The outbursts of moral indignation, the implicit self-righteousness of the commentators and the need for castigation will be extreme. The 'facts' will be obtained from children, young people and adults in the home identified as victims while their feelings of guilt, mystification or concern about the power of their own sexuality may remain untackled.

Sex in residential homes remains the Achilles' heel of social work practice even, as we have seen in Chapter 3, when it involves two adults who in any other setting would be allowed to enjoy whatever type of relationship they wished. In the absence of problems for management, sex is most often denied or repressed. When an incident comes to light, and there is any hint of unfavourable publicity or wider repercussions, a punitive response seems almost inevitable. As Righton suggests:

> It remains true . . . that staff are much more likely to be forgiven seven times for vicious cruelty to a resident than *once* for a sexual liaison with him – even when the relationship is fully desired and enjoyed by both . . . Provided there is no question of exploitation, sexual relationships freely entered into by residents – including adolescents – should not be a matter for automatic enquiry; nor should a sexual relationship between a resident and a worker be grounds for automatic dismissal.[2]

There is a great deal of confusion. Creating establishments which surround with suspicion so much that is comforting to those living elsewhere and then taking retributory action for rule breaking is incompatible with the philosophy of the caring profession of which residential social workers, practitioners and managers, form part. Unless we are able to broaden our approaches, we cannot be seen as very far along the therapeutic road. How would you approach the following?

> A slightly crippled, mildly epileptic girl, Maria, who is 17 years of age and of limited intelligence makes an apparently positive friendship with Bill, a single man in his early twenties who is employed as a gardener in the establishment and also works occasionally as a part-time care assistant during periods of staff shortage. Maria lives and works in this 'closed' establishment, has been 'protected' for several years and has no emotional links with the outside world, her mother having abandoned her at birth. The relationship between Maria and Bill is tolerated for six months while it seems to be at a superficial level, but one day Maria tells a favoured member of staff that she is having sexual intercourse with Bill.

There is no easy solution. Many opinions could be sought and as many solutions might be offered. The head of home, the homes manager, the committee members, the staff, even the other residents could bring influence to bear. Some organisations would require Bill's resignation (and later supply a reference which would make no comment about the reason for his departure), others would help the couple to arrange something for their chosen future. The foremost considerations must surely be the feelings of Maria and Bill and how they will be affected by any decisions that are made.

Whose problems?
Close relationships – sometimes involving sexual relationships – do result all the time in the need for decisions to be made about people and, when unpalatable facts are revealed, the management response is more often than not one of hurried dismissal – in both senses of the word – of those involved. For whatever reason, residential establishments can rarely tolerate 'pairings'. Difficult as these are between residents, they become impossible to manage between a staff member and a resident. Because many of these relationships are between adults, and the residents are not mentally handicapped within a legal definition, the solution lies either in formal disciplinary action; or in pressing the staff member to resign and 'clear out' quickly; or for the resident to be transferred; or for the staff member and the resident to arrive at their own decisions, which usually include the staff member resigning anyway.

Sometimes, of course, these relationships, and their resolution by the emotionally involved individuals, prove disastrous. On other occasions, two people may recognise within each other the sort of mutual attachment accurately perceived as right for them, and consequently have no concern for the administrative structures, management censure or 'what people say'. I am thinking of a young psychiatrist, Nigel, and a 19-year-old girl in a therapeutic community; of a female care assistant, Irene, and a physically handicapped resident; and of a probation officer, Rachel, and a man in his mid-twenties living in a probation hostel. Nigel and Irene found their own solutions by 'clearing off' with their partners. Rachel resigned, then waited for her boyfriend to leave the hostel. These relationships probably had as good a chance of working out as many others. But they had to be worked out outside the residential setting. Given the present frameworks of care I am not suggesting that alternative solutions would have been possible in these instances. What I am concerned about are, first, the messages conveyed to residents and other staff members about the nature and possible outcomes of close relationships, in effect very negtive messages; and, secondly, the way the residual feelings of those who remained were responded to. The swift departure of the staff members, and the residents, is a management decision. Do the perceptions of the 'solutions' of the remaining residents and staff members always run parallel to those of their managers? If not, has the work of the establishment been moved forward by the way that an incident was handled?

The speed and direction of the response may have something to do with the tightness and structure of the residential setting. Significantly, in less structured communities I have occasionally found the outcome to be quite different. In one old people's home a senior residential social worker, the third-in-charge, married one of the residents. He moved into her flat at the top of the building, he continued to be employed at the home, and the event was universally celebrated and accepted. From the moment the couple become engaged and the 'pairing' was recognised nobody seemed even to consider that the social worker should resign or be sent off 'in disgrace'. Similarly, such relationships have developed and been accepted in therapeutic-type communities where the emphasis is on working with present events and seeking solutions to them rather than making formal management decisions about despatching people in one direction or another.

The need for intimacy
What we do know is that strong emotional attachments similar to those described in this chapter will continue to arise. Having shared the pain of a number of people who have been caught up in similar relationships – which in almost any other setting would bring forth little comment – makes me feel that, for the most part, we still use very blunt instruments, too often concerning ourselves with amputations rather than the finer points of surgery.

There are bare wires running through every residential establishment along which pulsating currents travel. Anyone, resident or staff member, who makes contact or dares to approach too near may become a victim of the implicit or explicit labelling that swiftly takes place, even to the point of a 'criminal' tag being attached. This, of course, happens a great deal in work with children and young people, whether or not an allegation is made or an incident is brought to the surface within the context of a relationship between the young person and the adult.

Because of anxiety within the care givers about the possible outcome of close contact and close relationships with certain residents, work with some young people may be impeded. And staff members should be cautious. I have only to think of the loneliness of the head of home mentioned at the beginning of the chapter as he sat distraught in the centre of the room. But Malcolm, 10 years of age and living in a small community home, has a right to professional standards of care which cover the broad span of his physical, developmental and emotional needs. Malcolm's stepfather went to prison for indecently assaulting him and he subsequently made allegations against his foster father. He is small for his age, is constantly masturbating and frequently asks for and needs cream for his penis which is always sore. The boy makes close physical contact with male staff, enjoys their company and being bathed by them. Not unnaturally they are generally a little wary of the boy. One particular worker, a homosexual with a steady partner outside the home, feels particularly vulnerable. Yet Malcolm needs love, physical contact and primary care – from males as well as females – no less than any other boy in the home. He also needs close relationships with males who are not going to disappear from his life whenever he chooses to report that one of them has been playing with his 'willie'; and understanding as he grows through adolescence that sex is neither nasty nor dirty.

On account of his earlier history Malcolm seems likely to stay in the community home for some time. He may be there for several years. Without intensive intervention and involvement in the sexual side of his development Malcolm could become a most bizarre individual at 14 or 15 years of age. Many community homes, adolescent hostels and residential schools have one or more young people of this age for whom sex is potentially a totally destructive force. In Malcolm's community home the staff are working on a strategy to help the boy: being open about his behaviour and, more especially, talking in detail in group supervision about their own feelings and ways of responding to Malcolm when bathing him, giving medical attention or cuddling him. They need this discussion first and foremost for their own self-protection. While another allegation might prove disastrous for a staff member, it could be equally damaging in the long term for Malcolm. With his background he could become forever alienated from the only males able to give him the health-giving emotional experiences he so desperately needs for his overall development.

Power

In any discussion of sexuality in a residential setting we should include the subject of power. Although at a conscious level he is unaware of the extent of his power, a great deal in fact is invested in Malcolm. He has the power to destroy, but is probably unaware of it. At 15 years of age he could be using it to blackmail people. Some years ago a former colleague of mine had responsibility for the primary care of a group of adolescent boys. X will suffice for his name. It could have been argued that because of the boys' serious deprivation, or because they were growing adolescents, touch would play a part in caring for these boys. And we saw in Chapter 2 how important touch is in the developmental process. X believed and practised this, providing colleague-approved standards of care involving varying degrees of physical contact with the boys. He was in his late twenties, a respected worker and had a girlfriend of long standing. The swift outcome of an 'allegation' – perhaps in retro-spect no more than strong rumours among the sexually-loaded banter of the boys (it was always difficult to pinpoint the source of the comments) – was suspension from duty, police investigation and the suicide of X. Enquiries were never 'satisfactorily completed' and X's 'guilt' or otherwise never established. Indications are that any findings would have hinged on slender interpretations, the accusation originating from a stimulated, physically affectionate and active group containing all the minor jealousies and develop-mental anxieties of any such closely knit unit.

Touch was there, used and approved at colleague level, although given little importance or consideration by the head of the establishment. Sexuality was everywhere – within X, within the boys, within his colleagues – but perhaps most pertinent of all, neither recognised nor discussed by the head of home. This might say something about his own fears and reflects the shallowness of communication within the establishment, but in power he was supreme and could take the 'objective' decision to suspend X from duty, ignorant of the later unexpected turn of events. Or was it unexpected? The point to grasp perhaps is that power, or lack of it, became a central issue in this home. All of a sudden the power of the boys erupted – wittingly or unwittingly – and with dire conse-quences. Or was it the use of power by the head of home that was destructive? Or was the climate of the home reasonable by most standards and the power of X in hastening his own death of com-paratively minor and passing importance, an intra-personal conflict he chose to resolve in this way? There are no easy answers to these questions, as has been demonstrated by other, complex case examples throughout the book. Nevertheless, neither the boys nor the head of home will ever forget the manner in which they used their power, and the way in which X used his and consequently negated their own. Undoubtedly, as in every other residential establishment, the issues of touch, sexuality and concomitant power were vitally present in this inter-personal, intra-personal and organisational complex but the custom and environment neither allowed for the degree of progressive understanding calculated to avoid such (exceptional) tragedy nor for the use of the incident as a vehicle for learning.

I do not deny the complexities involved, nor the value of legal protection and legal proceedings on occasion. However, there is need to ask searching questions about the roots of certain 'problems' surrounding touch and sexuality, and to examine the nature of our responses. It is important to query sometimes whether there is a problem. Do we create difficulties and then reject the most heavily involved party because the residential unit is not in essence a caring community, no more being offered than benevolence and tolerance in return for major conformity? What machinery, we should ask, is there for *helping* staff day by day, staff always at risk of standing accused?

Allegations

Social workers do find themselves charged with offences, and court appearances are not uncommon. I have been involved in a number of these and one concerned a residential social worker in his late twenties who was cleared of ten charges of indecent assault against adolescent boys. The trial was stopped after five days when the judge dismissed the case. The court was told that the defendant was arrested when he went to the police station to help with inquiries about the head of the children's home where he had worked previously.

During the trial one boy told the court that his genitals had been fondled under the bedclothes; another said that a hair dryer had been pushed down his pyjamas. In his statement the defendant said that he did not remember fondling the boy ('I assume it was a light-hearted settling down for bed') and, giving evidence, he described rough-and-tumble play in the children's home: 'When I dried the boys' hair there was a lot of joking about. I put the hair dryer under their arms and between their legs. I'm not a particularly serious type of person and this was a situation where we were supposed to be relaxed. So I joked most of the time.'

The defendant admitted touching the boys' genitals to make sure they were clean: 'I only did it within my responsibility as their guardian. There was no sexual intention at all.' The local paper reported other details of the case: 'I washed the boys over a couple of months . . . As regards the sex book incident, I wished to show the boys what occurred and why. I thought it was necessary to show the boys what happened.' When asked about an incident in a holiday caravan the defendant said: 'Good grief, I never did that. I gave the young ones a kiss and a cuddle before they went to sleep.'[3]

In his concluding remarks the judge drew the attention of the local authorities concerned – there were two involved – to the seriousness of the issues which emerged during the trial in relation to their responsibilities for care practice in children's homes.

I was called by the defence as an expert witness and asked to put before the jury some of the problems of residential staff working with disturbed, unsettled, often unhappy and jealous young people. I spoke about the importance of touch, the nature of deprivation and the power of adolescent sexuality, pointing to the sexual rivalries which develop in group living and to the constant risks faced by staff operating in difficult areas of child care practice. A great deal – probably the outcome of the trial – depended upon the question of the sexual gratification experienced by the adult. The defendant was presented as an untrained worker holding a senior position, a man who worked hard to create a warm, friendly environment for those in his care. It was said that he 'always behaved professionally', and the trial would appear to have resulted from a lack of guidance, inadequately thought out care practice and unsupported, individual risk-taking.

In reply to questions I felt unable to reassure the court that guidelines for practice, supervision and staff training in many children's homes could be considered of a satisfactory standard, and it was admitted that decision-making in the grey areas was likely to rebound at some point on any individual who sought to work intensively with touch-hungry children.

I was pleased with the outcome of the trial but it seems important to acknowledge the anguish experienced by the defendant and his family during the weeks before the case came to court and, more especially, during the five days he spent in the dock. A conviction could have meant two or three years in prison. The boys, too, must have been confused. Some of the evidence underlined the strength of the relationships which had existed between them and the defendant. I wonder what opportunities were subsequently given to the boys for 'talking through' the accusations which brought about the trial and their appearances in court. Or was the matter so embarrassing to other adults that the subject was immediately buried? Again, as in the case of X, the boys will not forget their part in the proceedings. Discussions with them might have helped. In the wake of the judge's ruling, unfinished business remained: together with a number of bruised people.

Once more this case showed a residential social worker caught up in the complexities of care practice and, once more, it seems that the work of the children's home was perhaps not sufficiently monitored. What was the frequency of the individual supervision of staff in the children's home? Was there a forum for regular group discussion about the feelings of the staff? How often were there meetings for all children and staff? Was a consultant readily available? These questions should always be asked in the face of an enquiry, making some shift from individual accountability to collective responsibility.

Patterns of response

No subject raises such emotion as a suspicion of 'interference' in residential establishments. As we know, there are many 'scares', some accusations, and a number of resignations.

The most difficult statements from adolescents to senior members of staff must surely be: 'Last night when I was ill Mr A came into my room to take my temperature and put his hand on my breast' or 'When we were at camp on Saturday Mr Z came into my tent and played with me.' There are even greater complications when such a remark is made about the head of home to a junior member of staff. We are all on trial from that moment. Sitting down with a young person and asking for an elaboration of the statement means that the story is told without a witness. Often it is impossible to strike a balance between belief and disbelief as, at that time, the whole of the named individual's reputation and 'residential contribution' over the past years flash in front of the member of staff engaged in the interview. The absence of a witness may mean that the story has to be told on yet another occasion, each account reinforcing the previous one and making it more difficult for the young person to retract or to modify the original statement if he or she so chooses.

On the other hand, if it is decided to call in the person to hear the accusation first hand, the risk is run of embarrassing or inhibiting the young person so that he or she is fearful of telling the story.

Questions of suspension, whether to inform the police and what to tell the staff and other young people living in the unit arise immediately. I use the word 'immediately' because quick thought and instant decisions are necessary, even if the decision is to do nothing. The choice between not taking action and communication with others is in itself significant and can have repercussions for the member of staff to whom the story is told, the person against whom an allegation has been made and the adolescent. At worst, this decision may be the first step leading towards criminal charges and possible imprisonment.

Of one thing we can be certain: details of the alleged conduct will not be hidden from others in the building. Suspension more often than not carries with it some assumption of guilt, but from another standpoint, if an individual remains on duty, does this indicate to the young person: 'I do not believe you'?

Local authorities and voluntary organisations should have available, and frequently discussed and updated, a broad code of conduct for such emergencies, and the rights of each person involved should be widely known. But, of equal importance – and, I would hope, increasingly of greater importance – there should be guidance on how to lessen the trauma for all concerned. Under ideal conditions, I favour an immediate meeting between the young person, the accused adult and the staff member to whom the incident is reported. But such an approach can only be made in an open climate which supports the similar discussion of all other problems. Too few establishments operate at this level, and the risks in dealing with accusations in this way are great. More frequently, it seems better to see each individual separately in the presence of a witness acceptable to those being interviewed. It is difficult for a junior member of staff if he or she is spoken to first by a young person. In climates such as those created where Tina and Phil worked – incidents described in Chapter 2 – it may be necessary to seek outside advice before proceeding.

In general, the avoidance of suspension seems preferable, unless the person wishes to go off duty. Sometimes he or she does. The seriousness of the accusation will enable the individual to decide which course to adopt. From the young person's point of view it seems important to indicate that nobody is 'telling' anybody to go off duty. It must be remembered that frequently adults and young people who become linked in this way have previously had – and still have – an established relationship, and its destruction by formal and sometimes legal action can leave the young person with unbearable guilt about the part he or she has played. Caring for someone and then knowing that you have lost him or her a job, blighted a career, even forced a person out of their accommodation and broken up a family are heavy burdens for the 'victim' to carry, and often they have to be carried for a long time.

The sexual games and the sexual rivalries of children and young people are no less powerful than those enacted by adults. They may indeed be more powerful, lacking sophistication and thereby more readily ending, as we have seen, in accusation or blackmail. There are many young people in care who are well aware of their power over the adult through the use of their sexuality. Both boys and girls will employ it as the ultimate weapon in response to feelings of jealousy, frustration or deprivation. 'I can get you into trouble' is far reaching in its implications.

Resignation, the 'gentleman's way out', is like pleading guilty without a fair hearing, but occasionally a person feels that this is the right procedure. Sometimes, of course, for a head of home or a homes manager not to involve the police means treading on mined ground, but I do hear about incidents being bravely and professionally examined internally, putting into perspective the intensity of sexually-based interactions which are bound to happen within the intimacies of group living as the most complicated dyadic and triadic relationships are being worked out. Cases of exploitation and serious assault, although rare, will remain but the brutal and all-condemning nature of the proceedings associated with these incidents need not necessarily be extended to all others. The essence of residential work demands that, whenever possible, we should seek to heal and not to destroy, using each complexity of daily living as a learning experience. As was emphasised in Chapter 5, the manner in which an incident is approached can leave a greater scar than the incident itself.

Arguments are put forward for calling in the police at the first hint of a sexual allegation or a sexual 'scandal'. It is said that only in this way can bias be eliminated and the facts established – in fairness to all involved. Other agencies, as mentioned above, conduct some of their own enquiries, occasionally quite substantial enquiries, in the midst of great complexity, political pressures, individual soul-searching and a considerable degree of turmoil in the lives of the young people living in the particular residential home under scrutiny. The following edited news item from *Community Care* conceals the protracted anguish of several key figures in one social services department:

The enquiry into allegations about incidents in a children's home has, after evidence from more than 30 witnesses, concluded that 'all allegations were unsubstantiated or untrue'.

The social services committee accepted the 20–page report of the investigation into what allegedly occurred in its observation and assessment centre. A national newspaper had claimed that staff allowed youngsters at the home, including under-age children, to have sex.

It also maintained that one girl had had an affair with a married staff member.

A council statement on the report said it was possible 'to demonstrate substantial inconsistencies' through reviewing the material and contrasting evidence given to this and previous inquiries.

The council decided not to make the report public, because its substance and detail were 'confidential matters' about clients, ex-clients and council staff.

The enquiry was conducted by the director of social services and the assistant director for social work.[1]

Any allegations of this sort from any source are likely to bring to the surface very strong feelings – in managers, in staff members, in parents, in council members, in children and young people, and in the general public. Investigations are often of necessity lengthy, there is frequently a great deal of pain, embarrassment and bitterness, and nobody can ever be sure at the onset what eventually may be revealed. Disciplinary action may result. The police may have to be notified. Questions may be raised about the competency of staff at all levels. Politically, a 'sexual scandal' causes the greatest furore.

Staff support systems
In working with adolescents two important factors are made apparent throughout the many incidents described in this book: first, that from time to time allegations will continue to be made; and secondly, that there is a desperate need for guidelines for procedure and ways of minimising anguish and disruption. Because of the high level of sexual awareness and sexual curiosity of young people in our care; because of the emotional and bodily changes they are experiencing within themselves; and because of the unhappy childhoods many are just leaving, there is the potential for a great deal of destructive behaviour: to themselves, to their companions and to those who care for them. I feel that, in moving forward residential social work practice, and residential child care practice in particular, we are likely to provide a steady flow of defendants for the courts unless we take a much sharper look at what is entailed in working intimately – that is, in a way that brings about change – with children, young people and young adults in community homes, residential schools and hostels. On the one hand we have sexually aware, sometimes sexually active young people,

needing to understand more about their own bodies and to be educated in sexual hygiene and sexual responsibility. At a different, often child-like level, the same young people strive for adult affection, adult attention and the one-to-one relationships which they have frequently been denied.

On the other hand, what we offer to those working in the field, especially newcomers, is paltry in terms of alerting them to the delicacy of the balance required in responding to young people. Adults cannot set aside the impact of their sexuality and some young people, as suggested in Chapter 2, may interpret the most innocuous physical contact as a sexual advance. This is difficult when physical play, the importance of touch and the need for affection are universally recognised as essential elements in the care of children and young people in residential settings. With the age of puberty falling, with young people sexually active at a younger age, with sex education for youngsters becoming explicit and detailed, and with touch a rewarding way of making contact with inarticulate or distressed children and young people, managers must constantly examine the demands made upon staff as they engage in more adventurous caring.

I bring this chapter to a conclusion with two further case histories. The first, I feel, invites readers to think a little more about victims and offenders; and the second underlines the long-standing effects of both a sexual relationship and of the way that an incident was handled.

A short while ago I spoke to Tracey. She had left a children's home to move into a shared flat. When she was 15 she was found in bed with Tony, a temporary member of staff aged 19 years who was filling in the period between leaving school and going to university. He was dismissed, charged and convicted. Tracey's distress was considerable and no adult had yet been able to convince her that any man should be punished thus – or indeed at all – for having had sexual intercourse with her as a result of the fondness that had grown between them. Reports referred glibly to 'scandal' and 'assault' and justice was seen to have been done. Yet, are we able to speak of 'justice' when two lives have been so strongly affected by the aftermath rather than the act and as an outcome of overwhelming forces that would have operated regardless of the law or fear of its consequences? The onlookers saw fit to punish and destroy when neither person most affected by the proceedings could identify the crime allegedly committed.

The other example shows that female staff also carry the past with them. Mary, 32 of years of age and now working with her husband in a community home with education on the premises, recalls how 12 years ago she frequently had sexual intercourse with a 15-year-old boy, Clive, in the large children's home where she worked. The relationship continued for nearly a year after both had left the home. Clive and Mary parted amicably, the former to live with his married sister, the latter to a job in a different part of the country. Mary still thinks about that time, wondering what would have happened had they been 'caught' and even questioning the security of her present appointment 'should the department get to know'. Clive, she feels, found concern and comfort at a painful period of his life. Mary herself would not now encourage such a relationship – at the time it just 'happened' – but she remembers with affection the one senior member of staff in whom she confided before leaving the children's home. He chose to use counselling skill with both Mary and Clive rather than his power to destroy.

Sexual fears, sexual attractions and sexual taboos are stronger forces in the dynamics of group living than we care to admit. Often we fail to provide the meeting place where their complexities can be unravelled. The support systems we do offer rarely touch the edge of the dilemmas facing staff and residents. Each year the intensity of sexual feelings and experiences in residential settings results in a number of emotionally damaged and disillusioned people, those for whom everything has gone wrong. We cannot change the norms of society but we can display levels of understanding and tolerance unknown elsewhere. We can clear our minds of much suspicion, of the need to punish, and of the desire for excessive control. I am not celebrating the post-permissive society, lauding unbridled sexual activity and suggesting free sexual exchanges in residential care. I am advocating a hard look at institutional frameworks with a view to lessening the embarrassment, guilt, and harshness of response which surround too many aspects of sexuality in residents and staff members. But I go further than that, placing a responsibility on staff – again, both practitioners and managers – to display a far greater degree of kindness in working with events which, on first examination, may appear to merit retribution.

7 Sex, Social Workers – and Changing Values?

We are moving beyond the sexual liberation of the 1960s and 1970s into a post-permissive age where the western world is ordered by a new set of values: for example, sex education for 13- and 14-year-olds is explicit and detailed; contraception and contraceptive advice are more easily available to under-16s; short-lived sexual relationships no longer leave a natural burden of guilt; physically handicapped people increasingly assert their rights to a sexual life; homosexual relationships are more acceptable; the sexual needs of mentally handicapped people are slowly being recognised; living together is an alternative to marriage; and many elderly people expect to remain sexually active until late in life.

Field social workers cannot avoid becoming involved in the sex lives of their clients – in marital work, in upholding the rights of handicapped people, in working with more and more cases of sexual abuse, in supervising clients who have appeared before the courts for sexual offences and, as part of their social and professional responsibility, in helping to correct the often distorted and unsavoury perspectives on sex prevalent in some sections of the population. We have also been constantly reminded throughout this book of the ways in which residential social workers are likely to become even more closely, powerfully and sometimes painfully involved with the sexuality of those they live with and care for. There is no doubt that human sexuality is potentially the most destructive or the most satisfying force within man or woman, and through him or her in the wider social and economic worlds in which both operate. Hence its central place in social work practice.

To be most effective in facilitating the healthy sexual development of young people and in working with the sexually-related anxieties, misdemeanours and predilections of clients and residents of all ages in a variety of circumstances and settings I would suggest that social workers should:

* have a wide knowledge of the sexual aspects of people's physical being
* be aware of the sexual needs of both men and women
* be themselves on the road to sexual maturity

* have an understanding of their own sexuality
* be able to appreciate the joys of sex

* be knowledgeable about the sexual development of children and young people
* keep up to date with present approaches to sex education, and the ways in which children and young people learn about sex
* have a personal philosophy about sex and the under-16s
* be aware of the problems of the sexual abuse of children and young people, and the range of possible responses

* be able to recognise the sexual games played by both males and females, inside and outside marriage
* be familiar with the physical and emotional difficulties experienced by some people in sexual relationships

* have understanding of the special needs of handicapped people; of the sexual frustrations resulting from imprisonment, separation or injury; and of the particular difficulties faced by people living in residential homes or schools

* be at ease with people whose sexual orientation is different from their own

* have knowledge of the laws about sex, and keep abreast of current trends in prosecution and sentencing policy with regard to sex offences
* know where to obtain information and literature about sex and how to help clients and residents make contact with the various relevant agencies, for example, family planning clinics, rape crisis centres and special clinics.

Each of these areas, and I am sure that there are others immediately identifiable by readers, can usefully be expanded as part of a general statement about the specific knowledge, skills and understanding ideally possessed by social workers. However, as sex is such a private affair, the most intimate reflection, personal learning and the use to be made of the framework as an aid to practice, and as a preparation for practice, must rest with individual social workers. As a man or as a woman, a social worker, however well informed and sexually mature (and more will be said about sexual maturity a little later), will have a one-sided view of sex. Even in much less emotive parts of our lives it is never possible to enter completely into the world of another person. The demands on social workers call for movement beyond the 'personal' in a one-to-one free-flowing relationship unbounded by 'professionalism' and into diverse sexual worlds which, at a personal level, they may choose not to enter. In a private relationship it may take a long while to gain the maximum possible understanding of the sexuality of another individual. In a working role a practitioner may have to explore the sexual worlds of numerous people for comparatively short periods of time, and sometimes against their wishes. Therefore, it does no harm, I feel, before developing the themes outlined above to remind readers that *each response to the sexuality of a client or resident says something about the social worker and, at the same time, helps or hinders a man, woman, boy or girl in the development or expression of what for most people is a fundamental, vigorous and far-reaching force within his or her physical and emotional make-up*. The cumulative effect of numerous responses may have a far greater impact than at first appreciated.

Social workers should have a wide knowledge of the sexual aspects *of people's physical being*. They will, from time to time, find themselves working with clients, young or adult, male or female, who know very little about anatomy and physiology. Their problems may stem from ignorance: the help they need may be partly obtained by acquiring more factual information about how the human body works. In Chapter 2 one example showed how it was possible to help a resident. Eric, at 15 years of age, was simply unaware of the 'facts of life' although he had picked up, and was using, all the sexual words and phrases of boys of his age, and experiencing strong, accompanying sexual urges. The need for social workers to be well informed about basic sexual functioning is something more than having the knowledge base of an 'educated layman'. It should extend to questions of impotence, Caesarean births and venereal disease with particular attention being paid to the inter-relation of mind and body, for instance, in cases of masectomy, vasectomy, postnatal depression, hysterectomy and cancer of the testicles or womb. Work with clients and residents often focuses on the sexual and emotional repercussions of surgery, illness or disease and, while accepting that few social workers have medical training, it is important to be able to speak with some authority about the effects or the degree of malfunctioning associated with some medical conditions.

People are sexual beings. In *remaining aware of the sexual needs of both men and women* social workers need constantly to acknowledge this and to recognise how so much around them – in interpersonal exchanges, in the media, in the world of commerce – is a reflection of this sexual dimension. Sometimes, amidst the sordidness surrounding much that is brought to the notice of social workers – clients dulled by the effects of the unstimulating environments in which they are forced to exist and in the face of the gross handicaps and 'inadequacies' presented by some clients or residents – it is natural, and often convenient, to lose sight of sexuality. Yet the client will retain aspirations and have continuing needs, sexuality finding its expression in ways perhaps directly opposed to a particular social worker's own moral codes, upbringing and perceptions of 'normality' – or even decency. We know that some men engage in homosexual relationships in prison because, year after year, there is no other outlet for their sexuality. On release, most return to heterosexual relationships. People behave very differently in different environments. I have a vivid picture of Jill Johnson, aged 23, and the mother of three young children. The family lived in one room, the children sleeping in a large bed in one corner while their mother had a small bed behind a curtain in the other. Jill had a lover, the father of one of her children. The couple experienced a great deal of tension in their sexual lives, the very environment militating against intercourse except when the children were asleep. I am making no moral judgement. I am making no comment on the lifestyle that Jill had led since leaving school. What I am saying is that, at 23 years of age, she experienced herself as a sexual being and wanted to express this. Given her environment and her financial circumstances there was, in her mind, no other way of behaving apart from a denial of what to Jill was an important and valued facet of her personality. Deprived as a child she may have been, caught up in the poverty trap and perceived as 'irresponsible' from the security of a social worker's desk, Jill remained a sexual being. Who is to say how 'responsible' she might have been and what other opportunities she might have had for very different relationships within the warmth and comfort of the accommodation which most social workers have?

I do not believe in the notion of a fully mature sexual person. I do believe that *some people are further along the road to sexual maturity* than others, and that those furthest along the road are best equipped to respond to the sexual difficulties of clients. The fully mature sexual person is, I feel, illusory, the very nature of sex, sexual games, sexual play and sexual intercourse allowing and encouraging regression, spontaneity of behaviour, primitive and private verbal exchanges and role rejection. Sexual maturity may, therefore, best be measured by a person's ability to 'be' – and particularly in sexual exchanges and sexual activities – rather than to dominate, to fantasise or, as suggested in Chapter 3, to perpetuate struggles not yet worked out in other spheres of life.

We cannot all have every experience in life, and this applies to our sexual selves as much as to other parts of our lives. Social workers do, however, have a *responsibilty to maximise their understanding of their own sexuality*. Some who are called upon to unravel complex sexual strands within their clients will have had little personal experience. They may never have had sexual intercourse. Their advice, knowledge, understanding and empathy may only have come from reading, discussion and intellectual analysis. As one group of girls in a sex education class in a boarding school run by nuns said to the teacher: 'You have shown how it *is*, sister, but you haven't told us how it *feels*.' How could she? She was, nevertheless, a good teacher.

Other workers will have had a series of sexual exchanges, homosexual, heterosexual or both. They may, in the process, have had some of the accompanying emotional upsets which often stem from intense relationships. Gradually, either from reading and analysis or from personal experience, social workers will have built up their perceptions of sex: as something to be wary of, merely to put in the context of physical satisfaction, to issue warnings about, to regard as something to be avoided; or to see as having the potential for the fulfilment suggested at the beginning of Chapter 3. I know social workers, field and residential, who seemingly fall into one or other of these broad categories. In the very messy sexual arena in which social workers operate – rape, incest, sexual dissatisfaction in marriage, indecent exposure and allegations by children against adults (all from time to time intrinsically linked with violence and humiliation) – *the joys of sex* may be lost sight of. Most work with clients and residents must move beyond leaving them with feelings of the need to leave sex alone in the future to a point where they feel more comfortable with themselves as sexual beings and able to experience the joys of sex with the appropriate and chosen partner at the right time and in the right circumstances.

Social workers should *be knowledgeable about the sexual development of children and young people*. For example, boys do worry about the size of their penis, uncontrollable erections at the most embarrassing moments, nocturnal emissions or the slow growth of pubic hair. Undescended testicles are now usually noticed at quite an early age during regular school medical examinations. Occasionally, however, a boy will be admitted to a community home having missed out on an operation – through numerous changes of school, frequent absence, the constant movement of parents or having only recently arrived in the country. It is important to be aware of this possibility. Children and young people are sometimes more concerned about their bodily images than adults realise. Colin, living in a community home, started to truant from school, and especially from games lessons. He could not bear having showers with the other boys. At 13 years of age he had a tiny penis. Talking about this one evening with a member of staff just before bed the two were joined by a 16-year-old also living in the home. The member of staff drew him into the conversation. The older boy talked about the growth of his own sexual organ as he, too, in his early teens had been troubled about its small size. It took a long while for Colin to be reassured, to gain a little more confidence in himself as a sexual person equal to all others, but he was successfully reintegrated into school and into the physical education programme.

Menstruation presents problems to some girls. Period pains are often very real. There are undoubtedly changes of mood before a period starts and, despite preparation, young girls are afraid of 'leaking'. Hazel described the onset of menstruation:

> It came on early one morning. I went to my parents' room and woke my mum. Dad was asleep – or pretended to be. I whispered to mum, 'I think I've started.' She said, 'You'll find something in the bottom of the wardrobe.' I rummaged around, found the package and went back to my room. I wasn't very regular to begin with and was never quite sure when I was going to start. I used to worry about what to wear. I had a lovely white dress that I liked a lot, but I was always a bit afraid.

Just as Colin started to truant from games lessons because of embarrassment about the size of his penis, girls will occasionally refuse to take part in physical education – or sometimes to go to school at all – when they are having their periods. For some, there is considerable discomfort. Others just cannot tolerate the idea that fellow pupils should know.

Many parents, I am sure, are unaware of the content of the *sex education* courses in some comprehensive schools. The teaching is often excellent. Social workers, too, may have little knowledge about what children are taught at different ages. Improved awareness of the extent of their knowledge is important in working with young people in their own homes or residential settings. They may wish to discuss further some of the facts assimilated in the classroom. In one comprehensive school in which I was recently working the teaching for pupils aged 13 and 14 years was direct and detailed. Fully illustrated material was made available to all pupils and the following topics were included: sexual development; sexual intercourse; menstruation; masturbation; venereal diseases; contraception; pregnancy and sterilisation. Drawings showed a penis inside a vagina during intercourse; uncircumcised and circumcised penises; packets of contraceptive pills; intra-uterine devices; diaphragms; an applicator filled with spermicidal cream being inserted into a vagina; and where to find syphilitic sores on the sex organs. The following extracts from the text demonstrate further the frank way in which sex is now being taught to young adolescents, several of whom I found working seriously on projects on contraception:

Sexual intercourse: In simple terms, the man puts his penis inside the woman's vagina and leaves his sperm there. This obviously can't happen when his penis is hanging down, but when a man gets large and erect (pointing outwards and up) it can then go into the vagina. The vagina gets bigger, too, and so the penis can fit in it all right. The man moves his penis backwards and forwards in the vagina until he reaches a climax, when he 'comes' and shoots out sperm from his penis into the top of the vagina near the neck of the womb . . . There are many ways of making love. The best known one is when the woman lies on her back, her legs apart, and the man lies on top of her so that his erect penis can slide into her vagina.

Is my penis big enough? This is often a boy's biggest worry – especially as so many 'dirty jokes' are about the size of a penis. And here there's no need to worry at all. For an adult, the size of the relaxed penis often varies a lot – but when it's erect (ready for sexual intercourse) most men have roughly the same size of penis – and the actual size has nothing to do with how good you are at love-making . . . It makes no difference to your sex life whether your penis is circumcised or not.

Is my vagina normal? Between periods a girl will often have a slight white discharge from her vagina – this is normal. Also when a woman is sexually excited, the glands at the entrance to the vagina will make her very moist – this is to help 'making love' easier.

Does 'making love' hurt? Girls sometimes think that their vaginas will be much too small to hold an erect penis without it hurting them – this is not true. The vagina is so stretchy, it fits itself to the size of a man's penis – and also to the birth of a baby. But it is important, especially when a couple make love for the first time, that the man makes sure that the woman is relaxed and her vagina is moist, before he gently puts his penis into her vagina. In fact, 'love-making' is a very pleasant experience (if it wasn't the human race would soon die out!), although it's important to know that it may take much longer for a woman to become sexually excited – so it's up to the man to help the woman when making love.

Masturbation: Masturbation for a boy means rubbing or stroking your penis to produce sexual feelings and a climax – when you shoot out semen. After a climax, the penis soon goes small and limp again. For a girl, it means rubbing her clitoris. The clitoris is a small, very sensitive organ about the size of a pea which is in the front part of the soft folds of skin around the vagina. Rubbing the clitoris also produces sexual feelings and, maybe, a climax. Most people (including adults) masturbate at some time or another, especially during adolescence. It's not an unusual thing to do, and it's nothing to be ashamed of. On the other hand, if you don't masturbate, don't worry, that's quite normal too! But all the stories about masturbation are *untrue* – it does *not* make you blind, mad or sterile.

Many children and young people, therefore, now know a great deal about sex from an early age. The above extracts, drawn from material currently used with pupils of 13 and 14 years of age, show how they are helped not to feel guilty about masturbation, and indeed are given very positive messages about the pleasure to be experienced in sexual relationships. Interestingly enough, I could find no reference in the text to what the law says about the age of consent.

Social workers must, of course, *develop a personal philosophy about sex and the under-16s.* We know from the evidence presented in Chapter 2 that sexual activity is very common among young people aged 14 and 15 years. We also know that in some parts of the country the police rarely take action with girls of this age when the partner is just a few years older, although a warning may be given. I am of the opinion that everything possible must be done to avoid unwanted pregnancies. Some social workers, however, do find it difficult even to raise the subject of contraception with a 14- or 15-year-old girl. Sophie, in her mid-forties, has looked after June since she was 10. She is now 15. Sophie finds it almost impossible to accept that the child she has lived with in a community home for nearly five years is now a young adult capable of sexual activity, and of enjoying sexual activity. June has had a boyfriend for more than a year, the same boyfriend. They are known to be having a sexual relationship, but June would never be able to acknowledge it to Sophie who year after year has sown in June's mind the idea that 'nice girls don't do that until they are married.' June is a 'nice girl', she is devoted to Sophie and wants to preserve the relationship, but she does value the time she spends with her boyfriend. Working with Sophie it took extensive discussion to help her to accept the need to talk about contraception with June. Eventually she did. I don't *think* she was too late.

The more I come to understand adolescents and adolescent sexuality the less weight I give to the argument that young girls supplied with contraceptives are given a licence to have sex. I have greater respect for young people and their ability – with counselling available – to manage their own sexuality. They may have sexual intercourse with a number of young men as they move through adolescence. Very many do. Young people have always experimented sexually as they grew up. My stance would be, where a sexual relationship does occur, to offer maximum protection, maximum counselling where needed and an outlook which ensures that 'such an activity becomes a positive and constructive experience in the developmental process leading to responsible adulthood.'[1] Having stated this, however, I realise that, for a variety of reasons, some social workers find difficulty in being seen to be associated either with colluding in breaking the law or appearing to encourage sex for those under 16. This is one area of practice where the debate will continue. Nevertheless, in the United States this year approximately one million teenagers will become pregnant. About 40 per cent of these will be 14 years of age or younger. In England and Wales during the same period there will be over 1,000 live births to girls under 16 and nearly 5,000 abortions.

The other area of continuing debate is, of course, the *sexual abuse of children*. Numerous examples in Chapter 5 showed that, despite cases where very firm action and punishment are called for, many more are best worked with in other ways. Talking to a very large group of predominantly female social workers, mainly experienced practitioners, I was surprised – when perhaps I should not have been – at the number who drew no distinction between violent and non-violent sexual abuse. They quite sharply told me that all sexual abuse is violent and ought to be responded to from that position. Their attitude is echoed in recent feminist literature:

> . . . there is no reason why incest aggressors should be treated more leniently than [other offenders], and many reasons – in terms of criteria like danger, damage and deterrence for the sake of prevention – why they should be treated as serious criminals relative to other offenders.[2]

I cannot accept this as a general statement for all the reasons which emerge from a study of the examples given. Police intervention may remain blunt and uncompromising. Social work intervention must be from a different standpoint: in the knowledge that the issues and exchanges form part of the web that two or more people will continue to spin throughout their lives, and even in the absence or after the death of one partner.

What I do think that we need to acknowledge is that many boys as well as girls are sexually abused and, in cases of abuse by men, have to have resolved not only the repercussions of a sexual exchange with an adult but of a sexual exchange with a male adult, an added dimension in a largely heterosexual world.

In my opening comments I made reference to the work of Giarretto, an American bringing new understanding to adult–child sexual exchanges. Giarretto is not 'soft' but his philosophy shows a breadth of vision and compassion that social workers could profitably incorporate more solidly into their own work. In a personal conversation with Jean Renvoize he said:

> You have to recognize they're not *them out there* – they're my brothers and sisters. It's an I–Thou respect for humanity. We all have parts we would rather not have. If you do not respect each other as human beings, respect each other's intrinsic value and intrinsic viability, then we can't help each other – you see? And so our caring is very pragmatic, very practical. Uncaring, unbridled competition, adversary relationships are not practical . . . In other words, to put it bluntly, it takes a lot of people to screw these people up, and it'll take a lot of people to set them straight.[3]

More formally, he writes that his approach is:

> . . . fundamentally different from the medical model which tries to identify pathology or mental disturbances in the major role players of an incestuous situation . . . If I face my client busily trying to plug him into some pet theory, I defraud both of us of the rich potential inherent in an I–Thou relationship . . . The purpose is not to extinguish or modify dysfunctional behaviour by external devices or to cure 'mental disease'. Rather, we try to help each client develop the habit of self-awareness (the foundation for self-esteem) and the ability to direct one's own behaviour and life-style. But it is essential they probe the painful areas connected with the incest . . . I tell them that buried feelings (fear, guilt, shame, anger), if not confronted, will return as ghosts to harass them. If confronted now, they will lose their power to hurt them in the future.[4]

It is possible that as many as one child in ten will experience some form of sexual abuse within the family. Others will have early sexual experiences with adults elsewhere. Most will grow up into healthy adults capable of finding fulfilment in sexual relationships. A number will be deeply disturbed throughout their lives by incidents in childhood. I do not rule out punishment in cases of violent sexual abuse. Indeed, I see such a societal response as just and almost inevitable. My experience, however, is that from the moment of investigation societal violence may often be so strong that all involved are damaged or destroyed in the process.

We have already considered the *sexual games played by both males and females inside, and outside, marriage.* Dominian's list of 'excuses' on page 39 is an amusing yet serious example of the dramas played out nightly by couples everywhere. Any one excuse may engender anger or feelings of rejection. Mostly, however, the 'games' are harmless, leaving disgruntled partners of either sex to find satisfaction with others or in different aspects of their lives. Sometimes, however, the resultant frustration leads to wider marital disharmony – or is the avoidance of sex a reflection of this already? – and uncontrollable bouts of violence may erupt.

The whole concept of marriage, of intimate living bounded by a legal tie and shared property, of the 'rights' of a husband, of the responsibility for children and of economic dependency must in many instances be barriers to successful sex. All these are taken into the marriage bed each night, making more and more impossible for some couples the open relationship often present in their very first act of sexual intercourse. Perhaps this is one reason for seeking new relationships. At least they appear uncomplicated at first with the possibility of physical and emotional satisfaction of a much purer kind unencumbered by the accumulation of the other factors.

It is these emotional and domestic features that often creep into the *physical side of a relationship.* Very few men cannot get an erection, very few women fail to secrete moisture given appropriate stimulation and a relaxed emotional state. Most frequently, therefore, the mechanics of sex will look after themselves if what is contributing to the barrier is removed. Sadly, it is often marriage itself, and all that society has chosen to invest in it, which is the barrier, something that most social workers can do very little about – caught up in it as they are.

As we have seen earlier very many people have *special needs arising from handicap, physical isolation or merely living in a residential establishment.* A very high percentage of the population is affected in this way, perhaps several million people. What appears to happen is that sexual norms are determined, in general, by people who are able-bodied and have freedom of movement to express themselves as they wish. This freedom of movement allows for a high degree of choice – even for those who are married – in the expression of their sexuality. Adequate finance resulting from regular income at a reasonable level also facilitates choice. In exercising these advantages the able-bodied, self-regulating majority have gradually defined over time what is right or wrong, what is permissible or not permissible, not only for themselves and what they feel comfortable with because it meets their needs, but for all other sections of the community. As the needs and values of this power group have changed, for example, in respect of homosexuality, sex magazines, cohabitation and prostitution, so the boundaries of law and convention have been pushed back.

The levels of control that the power group imposes upon minorities are, in effect, still quite horrifying. And often members of these minorities are the clients of social workers. It would seem important to start posing a new set of 'in whose best interests' questions. What right have residential social workers to control – so strictly in some instances – the sexual lives of physically and mentally handicapped people? To determine which people will sleep together? To prevent a 16-year-old girl living in a community home with education on the premises from having a sexual relationship? If we are honest, is not the practice of prohibiting prisoners from having sex with their wives, perhaps for 20 years, a way of making their punishment even more severe? Why cannot adults in residential homes cohabit if they choose?

Answers to these questions based exclusively on the needs and wishes of the clients and residents principally affected would present a threat to the controlling majority – in terms of the types of accommodation made available, the values that may be upset, the arrangements to be made and the services to be provided. There would be a fundamental shift in the power base. Lesbian lovers and homosexual pairs behave in any way they wish in their own homes. Simply because similar couples have lifeless or twisted limbs and have to live as part of a large group in a residential home do we have any right to withhold from them the expression of their sexuality in any way they choose? Do we not have a moral obligation to assist them in their sexual activities if they have expressed needs? These are the further questions we should be asking. If we are serious about 'freedom of choice', 'freedom of action' and the 'rights of the individual' then we should not draw the line when we, the care givers, become embarrassed, confused or unable to cope with complex moral and emotional issues. For too long social workers have straddled both groups – the power holders and the minorities – living uneasily with the compromise between their personal and professional sexual selves. Many of those who seek to control the sex lives of others enjoy regular sex with the partner or partners of their choice. Has a man demanding sex from his wife each night any right to be critical of a head of home who assists two physically handicapped male residents to enjoy oral sex? Or to be critical of the residents themselves?

Social workers, at least, should be *at ease with people whose sexual orientation is different from their own*. From my observation and experience I would think that social workers have probably broken down as many barriers as any other professional group. But the problems are wider than this because 'It is not necessary to study this subject for long to discover that many people strongly disapprove of homosexual relations, whatever their views may be about the plight of homosexuals.'[5] The very use of the word 'plight' and the later quest in the *Working Paper on the Age of Consent in relation to Sexual Offences* for 'causes of homosexuality' show how many people continue to be prejudiced against homosexuals and would wish them to become heterosexual if at all possible. The working paper does make some concessions:

> We believe that the law has a part to play in bringing about acceptance of homosexuals by not discriminating unnecessarily against homosexuality. However, most of us think that the law should, as regards protecting young people, advance cautiously and while being compassionate towards the difficulties of those with homosexual leanings, should not attempt to take an exaggerated lead in seeking to change public attitudes to homosexual acts.[6]

I find unhelpful the use of the word 'difficulties' – whose difficulties, we may well ask? – and also later statements:

> One of the factors which often contributes to the unhappiness of the homosexual way of life is that sexual relationships between homosexuals usually tend to be short-lived and unstable . . . Possibly also promiscuity is more common among male homosexuals partly because men by nature are more promiscuous than women.[7]

What is significant about the working paper is the minority report, signed by five women. While the whole committee favours the reduction of the minimum age for homosexual relations to 18, the minority group would wish a further reduction to 16. Their last argument is the most persuasive:

> The law should not discriminate between male and female unless there are very strong reasons for doing so. A minimum age of 16 would put young men engaging in homosexual relations on a par with young women

engaging in either homosexual or heterosexual relations. It may be true
that psycho–social maturity is not achieved as early for boys as for girls,
but this does not seem to us an adequate argument for making them wait
for two years longer than girls before they can decide about having
homosexual relations. By 16 the individual should be free to make his
own decisions on these matters, as far as the law is concerned.[8]

Neither the British Association of Social Workers nor the
Residential Care Association gave evidence to the working group
so the 'official' stance of social workers remains uncertain.
Individually, I would have thought that social workers would have
supported the view of the minority group. Any other position would
surely indicate that there was some residual discomfort, even the
hope that a boy would still turn towards heterosexual relationships
instead of waiting two years.

Sexual conduct is partly regulated by *the formal and informal laws
of the moment*. Social workers should be well acquainted with these
and also have *knowledge of current approaches to prosecution and
sentencing*. The years between now and the turn of the century will
see pushes and pulls in opposite directions: on the one hand towards
greater control and punishment and, on the other, towards a far
more liberal approach. I am convinced that the latter will prevail.
Despite the temporary upsurge and popularity among certain
groups of the 'moral' lobby – especially in the United States – what
we are witnessing is an overthrow of a great deal of traditional
religious teaching (but not necessarily the religion itself), even
within the ranks of the Catholic Church; huge numbers of young
adults living together either before or as an alternative to marriage;
steadily rising numbers of single parent families, not wishing to be
otherwise; and vastly increasing sexual activity among young
people. These represent massive shifts of emphasis, ultimately
bringing about corresponding changes in the value base of the
majority. In the context of similar changes in Europe – in France, in
Spain, in Germany and in Austria – the pace will accelerate. We
have only to take as an example the manner in which attitudes to
contraception have changed from, say, ten years ago. All sorts of
condoms and spermicidal creams are on open display in chemists'
shops alongside cough lozenges and aspirin tablets, and few public
toilets for men are now without a slot machine, equally accessible to
adults and adolescents. In Vienna vending machines displaying
packets of contraceptives are now even more visible in the main
thoroughfare of the city, for example, in Mariahilfer Strasse.

Gradually, I feel, fewer and fewer prosecutions will bring about changes in the laws relating to the age of consent for both hetero-sexual and homosexual relationships, with a new framework possibly based on the concepts of 'unequal power base' and 'assault on the person' mentioned earlier. There will yet need to be the series of working parties and working papers, perhaps taking us into the 1990s, but changes will occur.

Meanwhile, social workers need to know *where to obtain information and literature about sex and sexual problems, and how to help clients make contact with various relevant agencies* able to be of service. A list of these will be found towards the end of the book. It will by now be apparent that with sex touching so many aspects of social work and with the rapid rate of change in both culture and practice specialist help and advice must, on occasion, be needed by clients and residents, and by social workers in their efforts to be more effective. Often it is the smaller agencies which build up the detailed knowledge and expertise, for example, about schoolgirl mothers, contraception, homosexuality or the sexual needs of handicapped people.

This movement towards new sexual freedom is, I know, frighten-ing to very many people. They see the descent of the human race into degradation as old values are rejected and new attitudes spring up. They offer as examples the most disgusting and nauseating incidents of sexual violence, sexual abuse and sexual perversion to support their case, doing nothing to convince themselves that sex need not necessarily be like this, and for many people *is* not like this. Sexual activity has, as I see it, untapped potential as a liberating force, as the most sensitive vehicle for people to come together as equals and for the expression of all that is good in a world where other forces – political, economic and religious – are in danger of driving people to patterns of behaviour which push sex even further into the squalid arena wherein they conduct a great deal of their other business.

Social workers, personally and professionally, have an exciting contribution to make in elevating sex in all its dimensions to the place I feel sure it was always meant to have in our existence, whatever the origins, purpose and futures of our physical, emotional and spiritual selves. However, what my experience tells me from working with individuals and with staff groups is that neither formal social work training nor the present levels of supervision and consultancy provide social workers with sufficient skills, knowledge and understanding to work confidently across this very broad field of practice. Yet, as we have seen, human sexuality is an ever-present element of their day-to-day work, will never 'go away' and must often be confronted and a resolution sought. Additionally, as illustrated by numerous examples in this text, it is quite apparent that, in matters of sexuality, a social worker's professional duty is almost bound on occasions to include, first, condoning or even encouraging breaches of the law and, secondly, ignoring agency policy. While I would be among the first to acknowledge the conflict and anxiety such actions may and do arouse, I would point out with equal determination that unnecessary suffering is caused by our avoidance, discomfort and mismanagement of this the most central of human affairs. The popular slogan 'Make love, not war' has much wider implications for the clients of social workers – whether in their own homes or in residential establishments – than are at first apparent.

Notes and References

Chapter 1
1. Proceedings of the Missouri State-wide Conference on Child Abuse and Neglect, Jefferson, Missouri, 30 March 1977
2. British Association of Social Workers, *A Code of Ethics for Social Work*, Statement of Principles, 6, adopted by BASW at its Annual General Meeting, Edinburgh, 1975
3. Most of the information in these paragraphs on the laws relating to sex has been drawn from Fact Sheet D.3 (32) published by the Family Planning Information Service, July 1981
4. Notes on decisions of the European Court of Human Rights, Strasbourg, *Forum*, Council of Europe, 1/82
5. *The Guardian*, 26 October 1982
6. *Working Paper on the Age of Consent in relation to Sexual Offences*, 1979, Policy Advisory Committee on Sexual Offences, Home Office, HMSO, p. 30
7. *Child Sexual Abuse*, 1981, The British Association for the Study and Prevention of Child Abuse and Neglect, pp. 8–9
8. Details of the law relating to mentally ill and mentally handicapped people have been taken, with permission, from *Getting Together: Sexual and Social Expression for Mentally Handicapped People*, 1982, MIND, p. 11
9. STORR, A. 1963, *The Integrity of the Personality*, Pelican, pp. 96–8
10. RIGHTON, P. 1981, 'The adult' in TAYLOR, B. (ed.) *Perspectives on Paedophilia*, Batsford, p. 24
11. DAVIS, L. 1982, *Residential Care: A Community Resource*, Heinemann, p. 66
12. SPENCER, S. 1981, *Endless Love*, Penguin, pp. 39–41
13. COUSINS, J. 1978, *Make it Happy*, Virago
14. *Problems of Children of School Age (14–18 Years)*, 1978, Report of a Working Group, Regional Office for Europe, World Health Organization, Copenhagen, p. 31

Chapter 2
1. See, for example, *Health Education in Schools*, 1977, HMSO, p. 118 and *The Times Educational Supplement*, 24 January 1975
2. *Problems of Children of School Age (14–18 Years)*, op. cit. p. 31
3. *The Times Educational Supplement*, 4 March 1977
4. *Problems of Children of School Age (14–18 Years)*, op. cit. p. 10
5. FARRELL, C. 1978, *My Mother Said . . . the way young people learned about sex and birth control*, Routledge & Kegan Paul, and quoted in *Pregnant at School*, 1979, Joint Working Party on Pregnant Schoolgirls and Schoolgirl Mothers, National Council for One Parent Families/ Community Development Trust, p. 13

6. STORR, A. 1968, *Human Aggression*, Penguin, p. 97
7. *Working Paper on the Age of Consent in Relation to Sexual Offences*, op. cit. p. 29
8. *Pregnant at School*, op. cit.
9. *Problems of Children of School Age (14–18 Years)*, op. cit. p. 9
10. *The Sun*, 21 June 1980
11. *Pregnant at School*, op. cit.
12. *Working Paper on the Age of Consent in relation to Sexual Offences*, op. cit.
13. Ibid, p. 10
14. *Problems of Children of School Age (14–18 Years)*, op. cit. p. 11
15. HAMILTON, M.W. 1962, 'Extra-marital conception in adolescence', *British Journal of Psychiatric Social Work*, vol. 6, no. 3, p. 117
16. BERNE, E. 1973, *Sex in Human Loving*, Penguin, p. 190
17. SUTTIE, I.D. 1960, *The Origins of Love and Hate*, Pelican, p. 64
18. Ibid. pp. 70–71
19. HESSE, H. 1973, *The Prodigy*, Penguin, p. 67
20. TRIESCHMAN, A.E. *et al.* 1969, *The Other 23 Hours*, Aldine, pp. 80–85
21. STORR, A. op. cit. pp. 33 and 34, referring to KINSEY, A.C. *et al.* 1973, *Sexual Behaviour in the Human Female*, Saunders, p. 704
22. DOWNES, D.M. 1966, *The Delinquent Solution*, Routledge & Kegan Paul, pp. 251–3 and noted in the chapter by MILLHAM, S. 1977, 'Who becomes delinquent?' in *Working Together for Children and their Families*, HMSO, p. 62
23. PEASE, K. 1974, *Communication with and without Words*, Vernon Scott, p. 30

Chapter 3

1. TRIMMER, E.J. 1970, *Understanding Anxiety in Everyday Life*, Allen & Unwin, pp. 73–5
2. DOMINIAN, J. 1968, *Marital Breakdown*, Penguin, pp. 79–80
3. The information in this paragraph has been drawn from Fact Sheet E.2 (36) published by the Family Planning Information Service, January 1982
4. McCARY, J.L. 1971, *Sexual Myths and Fallacies*, Van Nostrand Reinhold, p. 25

Chapter 4

1. CAMUS, A. 1942, *L'Etranger*, Librarie Gallimard, from the translation by GILBERT, S. 1957, Hamish Hamilton, pp. 83–4
2. SHEARER, A. 1972, *A Right to Love?*, The Spastics Society/The National Association for Mental Health, p. 1.
3. ISAACSON, J. and DELGADO, H.E. 1974, 'Sex counseling for those with spinal cord injuries', *Social Casework*, December, pp. 622–7
4. MILLER, E.J. and GWYNNE, G.V. 1972, *A Life Apart*, Tavistock Publications, p. 171

5. GREENGROSS, W. 1976, *Entitled to Love*, Malaby Press/National Fund for Research into Crippling Diseases, p. 22
6. Isaacson and Delgado recommend two teaching films: *Touching* and *Just What Can You Do*, obtainable from the Multi Media Resource Center in San Francisco
7. GREENGROSS, op. cit. p. 20
8. Advisory Leaflets, Association for the Sexual and Personal Relationships of the Disabled
9. *Sexuality and Subnormality*, 1972, National Society for Mentally Handicapped Children
10. GREENGROSS, op. cit. p. 20
11. *Getting Together: Sexual and Social Expression for Mentally Handicapped People*, op. cit. pp. 3–4 and p. 18
12. GREENGROSS, op. cit. p. 90
13. *Community Care*, 2 July 1981
14. *Social Work Today*, 11 August 1981
15. For example, *Social Work Today*, 8 June 1982 and 10 August 1982

Chapter 5
1. LAWRENCE, D.H. 1948, *Sons and Lovers*, Penguin (first published 1933)
2. RENVOIZE, J. 1982, *Incest: A Family Pattern*, Routledge & Kegan Paul, Chapter 3

Chapter 6
1. DAVIS, L.F. 1977, 'Feelings and emotions in residential settings: the individual experience', *The British Journal of Social Work*, vol. 7, no. 1, p. 26
2. RIGHTON, P. 'Sex and the residential social worker', *Social Work Today*, 15 February 1977
3. *Surrey Comet*, 16 December 1978
4. *Community Care*, 2 June 1982

Chapter 7
1. *Problems of Children of School Age (14–18 Years)*, op. cit. p. 31
2. NELSON, S. 1982, *Incest: Fact and Myth*, Stramullion, p. 73
3. RENVOIZE, op. cit. p. 202
4. Ibid. pp. 202–3
5. *Working Paper on the Age of Consent in relation to Sexual Offences*, op. cit. p. 14
6. Ibid. p. 20
7. Ibid. pp. 20–21
8. Ibid. p. 26

Additional references
The following references are all to articles by L.F. Davis in *Social Work Today:*

1978 'Sex behind bars', vol. 9, no. 37
1979 'A case of indecent assault', vol. 10, no. 24
1980 'The age of consent – is it time for a change in the law?', vol. 11, no. 19
1981 'Sex – is it just a dirty word in homes?', vol. 12, no. 37
1981 'Just a lesbian?', vol. 13, no. 10
1981 'Without prejudice', vol. 13, no. 14

Useful Addresses

British Pregnancy Advisory Service,
Aust Manor,
Wooton Wawen,
Solihull,
West Midlands B95 6DA
(Henley-in-Arden 3225)

A non-profit making
charitable organisation
London address:
2nd Floor,
58 Petty France,
Victoria,
London SW1H 9EU
(01-222 0985)

Brook Advisory Centre,
233 Tottenham Court Road,
London W1
(01-580 2991)

Centres also in Birmingham,
Cambridge, Coventry,
Edinburgh and Liverpool

Campaign for Homosexual Equality,
(CHE)
PO Box 427,
33 King Street,
Manchester 6
(061-228 1985)

There are also over 150
local groups in England and
Wales

Family Planning Association,
27–35 Mortimer Street,
London W1N 7RJ
(01-636 7866)

Local clinics throughout
England and Wales

Family Planning Association of
Northern Ireland,
47 Botanic Avenue,
Belfast B7
(Belfast 25488)

Local clinics throughout
Northern Ireland

Family Planning Information Service,
27–35 Mortimer Street,
London W1N 7RJ
(01-636 7866)

Grapevine,
296 Holloway Road,
London N7
(01-607 0949)

A free sex education advice
and information service
for young people

Health Education Council,
78 New Oxford Street,
London WC1A 1AH
(01-637 1881)

National Marriage Guidance Council,
Herbert Gray College,
Little Church Street,
Rugby,
Warwickshire
(0788-72341)

Local clinics

Pregnancy Advisory Service,
40 Margaret Street,
London W1
(01-409 0281)

London-based registered
charity

Rape Crisis Centre,
PO Box 42,
London N6 5BU
(01-340 6913)

24-hour emergency service:
01-340 6145

SPOD,
(Committee on Sexual and Personal
Relationships of the Disabled)
25 Mortimer Street,
London W1N 7AB
(01-637 5400)

Index